LAYMEN LOOK AT PREACHING

LAYMEN LOOK AT PSYCHIATRY

LAYMEN LOOK AT PREACHING

LAY EXPECTATION FACTORS
IN RELATION TO
THE PREACHING OF HELMUT THIELICKE

By

MARVIN J. DIRKS

THE CHRISTOPHER PUBLISHING HOUSE
NORTH QUINCY, MASSACHUSETTS

Most of the studies of preaching have focused on the message and method of the minister. In studies directed to listener attention and audience analysis the writer has come to feel that not enough attention has been given to the expectations of those who listen to preaching.

PREFACE

This book is the result of my continuing interest in speech communication in general and in the teaching of homiletics in particular.

Most of the studies of preaching have focused on the message and method of the minister. I have come to feel strongly that not enough attention has been given to the expectations of those who listen to preaching. My attention was directed to this area by a reading of a doctoral dissertation written by James L. Ray in 1962 at Boston University, entitled "Factors Affecting Lay Receptivity to the Preaching of Roy A. Burkhart." At the same time I was reading Dr. Helmut Thielicke's sermons and other writings. All of this helped to determine the nature and form of my study which in due time was called "Lay Expectation Factors in Relation to the Preaching of Helmut Thielicke."

During 1967 I spent a half year in Germany doing the ground work for the writing of a dissertation on this subject. This study brought to my attention so much that was interesting and that could be of value to others that I determined to bring it to your attention.

Without the cooperation of many fine people in Hamburg who were willing to lend their interest and assistance, the study could not have

5

been made. It is impossible here to mention the names of all those who helped or to adequately express my gratitude for all who willingly , cooperated in the study.

My deepest gratitude extends to Dr. Professor Helmut Thielicke and to Pastor Woldemar Lein for allowing themselves and their preaching to become the subject of research. Dr. Thielicke was more than generous in granting time for interviews at his home and at his Hamburg University office and in allowing his efficient secretary, Miss Louise Hinrichsen, to assist me in many ways, especially in making contacts with Thielicke listeners.

Perhaps no one was more important to the success of this study than Pastor Lein and Mrs. Lein (Kathy) and their able assistants, Sister Käte Gammelin, deaconess, and Gerold Brunson, a student assistant. Mr. Alfred Schroeder was most helpful in duplicating the "Interview Instrument" for the entire study.

A special word of recognition must go to The Rev. Oscar Wedel and his wife, Luise, whose help in translation of the Interview Instrument was invaluable. Dr. H. H. Harms (Hauptpastor), Pastor Adolph Gerber, and Miss Heika Schroeder, secretary to Dr. Harms, all of Michaeliskirche, gave valuable assistance at various stages of the project. Dr. Hans Goertz, a Mennonite pastor in Hamburg, at present a Professor at Tübingen University, gave freely of his time and effort in the final check on the translation of the Interview Instrument.

A word of thanks is due Mr. and Mrs. Harry Altmann for the use of a lovely apartment and for their quiet hospitality. I also owe a debt of gratitude to Helga Witteck of Hamburg for many hours spent in typing and in other ways assisting with the preparation of the original manuscript on which this book is based.

Finally, for their encouragement, constructive criticisms, and generous advice, I wish to express my gratitude to my good friends Dr. Herbert E. Stotts and Dr. Robert E. Luccock. And to Frieda, my wife, whose help and encouragement I value most of all, I extend my deepest appreciation.

CONTENTS

LIST OF TABLES

LIST OF GRAPHS

Chapter 1

LAY EXPECTATION FACTORS
IN RELATION TO THE
PREACHING OF HELMUT THIELICKE

The purpose of this book is to present a view of preaching that is usually glossed over in the training of ministers in somewhat the same way that basic needs and desires of family members are often ignored. Our purpose is to look at preaching from the point of view of the layman.

In a little book entitled *A Listener's Guide to Preaching*[1] William D. Thompson says to his lay reader, "Perhaps the expectations you bring have as much to do with the effectiveness of preaching as anything." This suggests not only that what the layman expects affects the preaching but also that the preacher ought to give thought to what the layman expects if indeed his preaching is to be effective.

Moreover, in an age of communication strategy, when laymen are accustomed to being bombarded from all sides with every kind of appeal, it is all the more imperative that we know what it is that most effectively moves the layman toward the purposes of the kingdom of God. Whatever may be our response to those who wish to ignore the impact of the communication strategy approach, the writer takes the position that it is both unwise and unethical for us not to take into consideration what the layman expects from his minister in preaching.

When teachers of speech or of homiletics use the standard communication formula of Who says What to Whom, When, How, and with what Effect, they are knowingly or unknowingly implying the existence of a whole constellation of *expectancy factors*. *Who* implies credibility and personality; *what* involves content, illustrations and originality; *when* involves or implies relevancy, preparation, and confrontation with decision; *how* implies delivery, continuity, and attention holding; *with what effect* raises questions involving delivery, inspirational quality, comprehensibility, and other factors already mentioned with who, what, when, how, and whom. The *whom,* of primary importance in our study, involves all the expectation factors about which the listener has opinions, feelings, or desires.

Keeping in mind that most of the listeners to preaching are laymen, both male and female, old and young, and that we are interested largely in the lay point of view, let us at this point set down a definition of *Lay Expectation Factors,* the central interest in this book. Lay Expectation Factors, as conceived here, are those characteristics of preaching most often mentioned by laymen as basic to their response to preaching. Lay Expectation Factors are those characteristics of preaching which have an effect, immediate or ultimate, upon the receptivity of the layman to the preaching of the minister. That is to say, these are the characteristics or the requirements of preaching which, when favorably dealt with by the preacher, make for a favorable response to preaching and for the desire to hear the preacher in succeeding presentations of his messages, and when unfavorably or ineffectively dealt with produce an unfavorable response in the hearer and are likely to discourage his attendance at successive presentations by the preacher. In this connection it must be remembered that the medium, in this case the preacher, is always a part of the message. Therefore, the preacher's personality must be considered as included under the definition.

Thus, the list of Lay Expectation Factors (L E Fs), which we shall present in due time, includes those factors in preaching which, when dealt with positively, actively engage the listener in Christian growth, in the work of the church, and in effect, in whatever involves him in the demands placed upon him by the preaching of the Christian Gospel.

Moreover, it shall be our purpose to show how the various lay expectation factors function in a successful preaching ministry. But

how did Helmut Thielicke become related to
all this?

By a series of events which shall not be reviewed here but which today seem more than
just happenstance it became the rare privilege
of the writer to go to Hamburg, Germany to
study lay expectation as related to the preaching of Dr. Helmut Thielicke. As a matter of fact
it was difficult at times to keep clearly in mind
the purpose of devising and testing a method
of study of Lay Expectation Factors from the
purpose of learning from Thielicke whatever
is to be learned from the preaching of a great
and good man. It must be added that much of
what follows first became a part of a doctoral
thesis completed at Boston University School
of Theology in 1968, the year following a six
month period of work on its development in
Germany.

The fact that the writer had listened to much
German preaching during his childhood and
youth had something to do with his ability to
pursue the study of L E Fs in Germany.

But why was Helmut Thielicke chosen to be
central in a study of L E Fs (Lay Expectation
Factors)?

(1) He has attained wide distinction as one
who proclaims the gospel in terms understandable to modern man and as one who is
concerned with communicating the living contemporary Word.

(2) His writings on widely different subjects

and his printed sermons are available for study.

(3) It was thought that more could be gained from the study of the preaching of a man known as a highly successful preacher than from the study of a less successful preacher.

(4) Also, since Helmut Thielicke is not a pastor, the response to his preaching was thought to be more completely related to preaching than the response to the preaching of a pastor would be.

If any one of the above four points was more determinative than the others in the choice of Thielicke and his listener response as central in this study, it must be point four. Because of the desire to direct the scope of the study as much as possible to the response to preaching rather than to the response to the total work of the pastor, the choice of Thielicke, a preacher who is not a pastor, was thought to offer definite advantages. Listener response, for example, would not be influenced by rapport gained from pastoral calling, nor would the response be negatively affected by any possible unfavorable personal contacts. All this is not meant in any way to discount the other three important reasons for the choice of Thielicke as central in the study.

Methodist Pastor and His Listeners Chosen
for Comparative Study—

From the time of the choice of Thielicke as

central in the proposed study, the plan also required the selection of a preacher-pastor and his listeners in Germany for the purpose of testing the interview instrument which had been developed in pre-tests in the U.S.A. It was decided that the control church should be a free church (not a State Church), preferably a Methodist Church, for in the free churches, especially in the Methodist Church of Germany the pastor-listener relationship is very much like the pastor-listener relationship in the Protestant Churches in America.

Pastors and interested laymen encouraged the selection of Pastor Woldemar Lein and the Methodist Church known as Christ Church (Christuskirche) in the Hamm subdivision of Hamburg. After a second visit to the regular Sunday morning service and after one private conference with Pastor Lein the selection of this church as the control study church was assured. As a participant-observer in the life of this Methodist Church the writer became much aware of the advantage of studying the preaching of Pastor Lein and the responses of his listeners for purposes of comparison with the results of the Thielicke study. The similarities between Christuskirche and the many Protestant churches known by the writer in the United States of America became a matter of personal experience to him.

On the other hand, the situation in the majority of the Evangelical Lutheran (Staatskirchen) churches in West Germany is very different from that in the American churches. The chief difference consists in the absence of a substantial adult participating congregation in the German Lutheran churches in which the Sunday morning congregation consists for the most part of catechumens between the ages of 13 and 16. Pastor Lein's congregation, on the other hand, looks very much like the congregation in the more active American Protestant churches.

Because of these and other basic differences it was thought that inferences made on the basis of the study of Thielicke listeners *and* Lein listeners might be more valid for American Protestantism than inferences made solely on the basis of a Thielicke study or on the basis of a study of Thielicke listener response compared with the listener response to one of the many able Evangelical Lutheran pastors in one of the Hamburg churches of that confession. Finally, it was hoped that inferences drawn from the study as conceived might be applicable to the preaching of pastors as well as to the preaching of men who, like Thielicke, are not pastors.

The preaching of Helmut Thielicke with which we are concerned was primarily that done in St. Michaeliskirche in Hamburg, Germany. American and English readers may know this great church as St. Michael's. We shall have more to say about this famous church and how it is related to the preaching ministry of Helmut Thielicke. Meanwhile, the reader is aware that even though this book centers on the response to the preaching of Helmut Thielicke, it includes for the purpose of comparison a study of the response to the preaching of Pastor Lein. Our question becomes "How do Thielicke and Lein, whether consciously or not, deal with the L E Fs and how are they related to the reception of the preaching of these men by their respective listeners?" In other words, how do laymen, in terms of the L E Fs, respond to the preaching of Thielicke and Lein? So although the *primary problem of the research* behind the writing of this book was to ascertain the importance of the *lay expectation factors* in the receptivity of listeners to the preaching of Dr. Helmut Thielicke, its actual scope is somewhat more inclusive.

Preliminary Problem of the Research—

In line with the purpose outlined and the assumptions made, the preliminary task the writer set for himself was to revise and verify the list of *characteristics of preaching repeatedly mentioned by laymen as basic to their response to preaching,* herein for brevity sake most often called *Lay Expectation Factors* (L E Fs), and to arrange this list into a hierarchy indicating comparative importance in the estimation of laymen.

How was this to be done? Methods often used in communication research, such as analysis of style of delivery and content analysis could be used to study the spoken and written forms of the sermons of Dr. Thielicke or of anyone else, but to study Lay Expectation Factors in relation to preaching required appropriate methods apart from the usual communication research forms. What was needed was a method of rating and comparing characteristics of preaching that would assign comparative values to the L E Fs chosen for evaluation, and that would also serve as a method of evaluation of the individual layman's response to the preaching of Dr. Thielicke or of any other preacher.

It was known that sociological and psychological studies had made use of what is known as the *Q-sort* method with considerable success. The Q-sort has most frequently been used in the study of personality, for example, in studies of changes in an individual's image of himself, of his ideal person, and of the actual person. The similarity between the use of the Q-methodology for self ratings and its use by the layman in ranking his expectations in regard to characteristics of preaching was quite evident.

For any reader unacquainted with the Q-sort method of rating a given list of characteristics, perhaps the easiest way to understand its use would be to turn to Appendix A, Page

300, for a look at the first Q-sort Test page as used in this study. On this form the listener is asked to rank the twenty separate factors into four equal groups from *most important* at the top of the page to *less important* on the lower fourth of the page. No difference was indicated in the importance of items within the groups of fives by the individual doing the test. The twenty characteristics (L E Fs) were written on twenty slips of paper and could be arranged and rearranged until the person doing the test was relatively satisfied with his evaluation. It is noteworthy that all but one or two persons interviewed found this a rather interesting and challenging process. Some accomplished the task in five minutes, while others took as much as a half hour of time.

Twenty Lay Expectation Factors

Why twenty L E Fs rather than sixteen or twenty-four or more? In 1962 James L. Ray was responsible for the writing of a Doctoral Thesis at Boston University entitled "Factors Affecting Lay Receptivity to the Preaching of Roy A. Burkhart." In his study James Ray had developed a list of *thirteen factors affecting lay receptivity*. This list was used as a starting point in the development of our more inclusive list of twenty factors.

In scores of interviews, by submitting selected expanded lists of lay expectation factors to individuals either in groups or singly, the present writer was convinced that Ray's list though adequate for his purpose would have to be enlarged in order to be inclusive enough to include all of the important factors. In systematic pretesting a list of sixteen L E Fs were submitted to 100 subjects from various denominational groups in the form of a Q-sort test. These included members of Methodist, Baptist, Nazarene, Mennonite, and other groups, mostly in the Boston and Quincy Massachusetts area.

Each person was asked to arrange the sixteen items in four groups of four each in order from *most important,* through *very important, important,* to *less important.* At the same time each person was asked to add any additional factors which he felt were either more important or at least as important to his reception of preaching as any of the sixteen factors submitted by the researcher. Of those suggested most often, four were eventually added in the actual testing programs in Germany.

In listing and evaluating the numerous suggestions of the laymen a problem of major proportions was the necessity of including under a very limited number of fairly precise headings the many suggestions made. The layman's suggestions most often came in the form of questions. For example, "Do his sermons help me in my daily life?" Or, "Is he aware of my needs?" "Does he relate the Bible to my needs?"

On the following pages is the list of Twenty
Lay Expectation Factors together with the definition of each in terms of what they meant to
the laymen who suggested them and to those
who eventually, through the Q-sort arrangement, provided the data by which we have
listed them in an ideal order of importance. In
succeeding steps we used these same definitions as a basis for the evaluation of the response of the listeners to the preaching of
Thielicke and Lein.

Even to list them alphabetically and to define them in this way is to risk being imprecise
to some degree. But this is what we are dealing
with in the use of the Q-sort method, an instrument that does not depend on precision of
definition. Even though we have striven for
the best definitions possible, there is much
overlapping and perhaps some duplication
among the factors.

The definitions are put into the forms in
which they came from the laymen. As indicated the list is arranged alphabetically.

20 LAY EXPECTATION FACTORS
AS EXPRESSED BY LAYMEN

Attention holding.—Does he hold my attention, my interest?

Authority, basis and use of.—What is his
authority based upon? Does he speak in the
fullness of power? Who are his authorities? Does he act as if he is the big authori-

ty? Does he speak with conviction? This covers the whole question of the source and the use of authority.

Bible, use of the.—Are his sermons biblical? How does he use the Bible in his sermons? Use of text, explanation of biblical background and the minister's attitude toward the Bible are all involved in the layman's evaluation of the minister's use of the Bible.

Comprehensibility.—Can I understand what he says? Does he use strange words, words he does not define? Does he explain his meaning in language I can understand? Does he speak distinctly?

Continuity.—How well is his sermon organized? Does it follow a logical development. (In German the term used was *Folgerichtigkeit.* It was perfectly understood by everyone.)

Credibility.—Can I believe what he says? Can I trust him? Does he know what he is talking about?

Decision, confrontation with.—Does he confront us with the necessity for making decisions about important matters? Does he lead us to make our own decisions? Are we confronted with the imperatives of the gospel?

Delivery, manner of.—Here style, format, fluency, intensity, and the entire matter of pulpit demeanor comes into question. Do I like his manner of delivery? Is his voice pleasant or unpleasant?

Illustrations, use of.—Are his illustrations effectively used? Choice of illustration and presentation of the illustration can not be separated in the mind of the listener. Are there enough interesting and effective illustrations? Occasionally someone asks, "Are there too many illustrations?"

Inspirational quality.—Does he inspire me? Can he inspire me to do what he advocates? Is he really vitally concerned with what he is saying to the point that I become emotionally involved in it? Does he involve me emotionally as well as intellectually?

Love-fear (quality of motivation).—How does he seek to motivate us? Does he draw us with love or does he more often use fear and anxiety as the basis of motivation? Is his approach psychologically sound? Do I feel that he is thoroughly Christian in his approach? Some laymen ask, "Does he hit us over the head with the Bible?" Is there a balance between the elements of love and fear?

Originality.—Is he original in his ideas and in their development? Does he bore us with old worn out phrases and ideas? Is he an original thinker? Do his ideas come to us clothed in new and interesting forms?

Practical help for living.—Do his sermons help me in my daily life? Is he aware of my needs and does he help to meet my needs? Does he help me face my problems? Does he help me to live a Christian life?

Preacher's personality.—Does his personality support his message? Is he a live, vital, interesting person? Does what I know about him support or detract from the quality of his preaching?

Preparation.—Do his sermons show evidence of adequate preparation? Do I feel that he has tried to prepare a good message? Does he really work at his preaching?

Prophetic voice.—Does he have a message for our times? Does he call us to repentance? Is he a modern Amos or Jeremiah? What does he have to say about the problems of our time? Is he concerned about the condition of the church?

Range of subjects.—Do his sermons include an adequate range of subjects? Does he avoid certain subjects? Or, does he change texts but continually speak on the same themes over and over again?

Relevancy.—Does he deal with relevant subjects in a relevant way? Is he in conversation with his people? Does he speak to their current needs? Is he sufficiently existential in his approach? Does he deal with needs appropriately as they arise?

Theological content.—Do his messages have an adequate foundation in theological truth? Do they contain sufficient basic Christian teaching? Are they doctrinally sound, true to the Bible? Is his theology related to living issues?

Thought provoking.—Are his sermons intellectually and emotionally challenging? Does he cause me to think, not only at the time but also later? Does he cause me to do some thinking on my own? Do I want to discuss what he talks about with others?

The *Q-sort* proved to be an effective tool for it provided a rank-order kind of evaluation of the *Ideal Lay Expectation Factors* and a descriptive view of the preaching of the ministers to whom the laymen were asked to respond in the Q-sort test. However, something more was needed for the purpose of evaluating the presence and the comparative strength of the L E Fs in the preaching. Why was this necessary?

There is a sense in which the Q-sort provides a partially distorted view of the value of the characteristics included in the list. The Q-sort is a "forced" test in that the listener is asked to rate the characteristics in four equal number groups when by his own inclination and by his own best judgment he might rather rate the characteristics in unequal groups. For example, when presented with the Q-sort on Thielicke's preaching (See Appendix A, Page 301.) the typical interviewee might say, "But he does them all very well. What will I put in the low group?" He would nevertheless proceed to arrange the items and would find some characteristics of less importance to the effectiveness of Thielicke's preaching than others placed higher up. Thus the inherent problem with the Q-sort as a measure remains.

Q-sort Augmented by a General Preaching Characteristics Test—

So it was that a General Preaching Characteristics Test providing scale value scores was devised to give us a cross-check on the L E Fs of the Q-sort List. Readers acquainted with research methods will recognize that the test used involves a variation of the *Likert* method. The Likert involves a scale-discrimination technique in which the listener is asked to choose on a given item *to what extent* the characteristic involved is present. In our test a series of sixty statements descriptive of effectiveness in preaching or of action in preaching was developed. Each of the statements, with few exceptions as seen in Appendix A, Pages 302-304, is related in some degree to one or more of the L E Fs. The listener's response to each statement was made on a five point scale representing a continuum ranging from "almost always," through "frequently," "occasionally," "seldom," to "almost never," to be scored respectively 4 - 3 - 2 - 1 - 0.

Thus, built into the test instrument was the possibility that characteristics ranked low in the Q-sort test by laymen might be ranked high in the Likert-type test, in effect making it possible to correct a partially false picture derived from the Q-sort program.

For readers who may be interested, Table 1 in Appendix B, on page 311, gives a list of the *Twenty Lay Expectation Factors* with indication of the numbers of the items in the General Preaching Characteristics Test relating to each factor.

On the last pages of the interview instrument were added a series of statements, questions, and classifications designed to elicit the necessary demographic data to be correlated with the information derived from the L E F testing. Those interested may again turn to Appendix A.   Information was collected on age, sex, occupation, education, place of residence, and the like, and the number of times the subject had heard the minister preach.

Space simply forbids an account of the conduct of the research in detail or even the description of the problems inherent in the necessity of translating the interview instrument into German. Our aim in translating was to find German terminology which would preserve the original intention and meaning of the American instrument and at the same time avoid the German feeling, "I understand it, but that is not the way we say it." At the end of six weeks of cooperative effort the document was approved grammatically and linguistically by competent German scholars, and the writer was satisfied that the entire instrument was effectively translated.

Of the twenty L E Fs, the most difficult phrase to translate proved to be *inspirational quality*. The difficulty was not so much linguistic as it was emotional. It was finally agreed that *Fahigkeit zur Begeisterung* was the nearest equivalent available, even though some stigma of disapproval may still be attached to the term *Begeisterung* because in the last war it was often used in connection with Hitler's speeches, where it was used much as we might say "He can inspire a person with his speeches." Many persons interviewed indicated that the term *begeister* could have good connotations or bad depending on the context. So *Fahigkeit zur Begeisterung* was used. Interestingly, in the Q-sort, Methodists in Germany rated this particular L E F nearly as high as any group in the pretesting in the States.

Additional Resources for Study

Interviews with Dr. Thielicke—

No one was more sympathetic or more co-operative to the purpose of this study than Dr. Thielicke himself. His remark "This is the kind of study that ought to be done," made at the conclusion of the first interview, was typical of his attitude. He appreciated the fact that our interviews could be carried on for the most part in the German language. His interest may be seen in the fact that the writer was granted a second extended interview and was invited to participate in several seminars with select groups of graduate students with Dr. Thielicke. He instructed his secretary to aid the writer in any way possible, for example, in making a collection of his writings and in contacting listeners.

Pastor Lein, with the support of his Church

Board (*Vorstand*), made possible my full participation in the life of the *Christuskirche*. Woldemar Lein's best contribution consists in the fact that he allowed himself and his sermons to become the center of investigation in the control study in Germany. Also, at his suggestion, the writer was given the assistance of Sister Käte Gammelin, Deaconess, and of the student assistant pastor, Gerold Brunssen, in the preparation of the membership list of Christuskirche, and for help in making appointments for interviews with members.

Publications Used in the Study—

Most important for this study are the books published under the authorship of Dr. Thielicke. There is an ever-growing list of titles, several of which have been published since the study upon which this book is based was made. The writer is in possession of a tape-recording of the last sermon of Thielicke's series entitled *How Modern Should Theology Be?* which he heard at Michaelis on February 11, 1967. Subsequently, this recording was translated into English and carefully compared with Thielicke's printed text of the message.

Chapter 4 will be given to a brief study of the sermon volumes and other publications by Dr. Thielicke.

Newspaper and magazine articles provide valuable commentary on the work of Dr. Thielicke in relation to the purpose of this book.

For the most part editorial and journalistic comment has been highly favorable to Thielicke. However, a group of alert young pastors in the Evangelical Lutheran Church of the Flensburg area (North Germany), who publish a religious monthly magazine under the title *"Zwischen den Zeilen"* (Between the Lines), have written a number of articles critical of both content and style of Thielicke's preaching. We shall attempt to incorporate ideas from these and other articles in the chapters on the writings and the sermons of Thielicke.

Field Techniques

The basic field technique was the interview in which the test instruments already introduced were used. How were the interviewees chosen? In the *control study* the availability of a membership list made possible the selection of interviewees on the basis of a *random* sampling according to standard research practice. This list of interviewees proved to be highly representative of the alphabetized membership list in regard to age, sex, and occupational classifications.

Sampling of Thielicke Listeners—

Almost immediately upon his arrival in Germany the writer discovered that there would be no way to get a sizeable list of names of people attending any given preaching service in which Thielicke was the preacher. Thielicke did not want his listeners to feel that he was in any way responsible for initiating a study of his listeners' response to his preaching. He was, however, in favor of compiling a list of names of listeners by any indirect plan that could be devised.

The following plan was used to develop a list that would be as representative as possible of the various groups or categories of Thielicke listeneres. Church secretaries, pastors, and friends (including those at Michaelis and Christuskirche, and including Dr. Thielicke's secretary) were asked for names of people known to have attended Thielicke preaching services at least two or more times. These informants were specifically asked to find names of listeners from the lower educational and occupational attainment groups as well as from the middle and upper level groups. Then, after the interviews with Thielicke listeners began, the interviewer himself asked each interviewee for additional names of known Thielicke listeners. The attempt was made, with some success, to find a number of people known to be critical of Dr. Thielicke's preaching, who might consent to be interviewed.

The population sample of Thielicke listeners as compiled and interviewed will be described in Chapter 2. Meanwhile, the reader should be aware of the fact that making such a list and making contacts leading to interviews with persons on such a list was very different from making successful contacts with members of Christuskirche, where one was given the feeling that he was offending those not asked for interviews. Pastor Lein eventually was asked to explain to the congregation how the sample was chosen and why not everyone was being interviewed.

The Interviews—

In the actual process of interviewing the first Q-sort task was presented to the listener before he was given the opportunity of seeing the remaining pages of the instrument. He was told that he was, in a sense, describing his own *hypothetical ideal preacher.* Brief standard definitions of each of the terms, as given herein on pages 28 to 31, were used in answer to questions about the meaning of the various L E Fs.

On page two (the second Q-sort) the procedure was the same, excepting that the listener was told "This time you have the preaching of Dr. Thielicke (or Pastor Lein) in mind. Which of the 20 L E Fs are most important to you in your response to *his* preaching? As before, you begin with the most favorable at the top of the page."

If the interviewee for whatever reason held a somewhat negative view of the preaching, as happened a few times, it was necessary to add, "All right! Just begin at the bottom of the Q-sort page with what you feel he does the worst."

Unless the process of completing the instrument was interspersed with a coffee break or with some similar diversion, the interviewee proceeded immediately to the G P C Test. With most interviewees few additional instructions were needed. When clarification was given, hopefully, it was given in such a way as to leave the subject entirely free to make his own choice. He was from the beginning assured that his anonymity would be respected.

The final pages were usually completed in from five to ten minutes. The completed interviews lasted from twenty-five minutes to, as in one case, three hours.

Many interviews were interspersed with or followed by conversations related to the research as well as to other unrelated matters. The attempt was made to remember and to subsequently record material pertinent to the study. These notes on the interviews provide instructive and valuable insights on the layman's response to preaching.

No space is allotted here for an explanation of the statistical procedures of the study. Anyone interested in this aspect of the study is encouraged to refer to the Th.D. Thesis under the same title as this book as available in microfilm or zerographic copy from University Microfilms, Ann Arbor, Michigan.

NOTES AND REFERENCES

[1]William D. Thompson, *A Listener's Guide to Preaching,* (Nashville: Abingdon Press, 1966), p. 40.

Chapter 2

THE CHURCHES AND THE
POPULATION SAMPLES

To understand more fully the significance of the results of our study of L E Fs the reader is now to be introduced briefly to the churches and the people involved in the study. Hopefully it will be helpful to include also a much abbreviated account of the origin and background of the churches and to describe the total population base as found in the city of Hamburg and therefore in the Thielicke and Lein listening audiences. Finally, we shall describe the people actually interviewed. This chapter must also include an introduction to Pastor Woldemar Lein. Let us begin with the church of which he is the pastor.

Christuskirche

The first group in Hamburg to be known as Methodist was founded in 1851. Its first chapel was built in 1890 near the central railroad station. As the city developed this location became untenable. A new church was built in the Hamburg-Hamm area. By 1927, when the new church was completed, there were four Methodist churches in Hamburg and the mother church in the Hamm subdivision was considerably weakened by the dispersion of Methodist membership into four churches.

In 1943 the Hamm church fell under the heavy bombing of the Second World War in which the entire section of the city, although largely residential, was destroyed. The church was homeless and the remaining members moved their services from place to place. Eventually plans were made to build the present place of worship on a new location in the Hamm subdivision and the new building on Carl-Petersen-Strasse 59 was dedicated in December of 1958.

Christuskirche is a united church in more than one sense. It is made up of members from two churches made homeless by severe war losses. A second place of meeting in what at present is functioning as a Methodist Youth Center is located at the entrance to the site of the old Barmbek church. A third place of meeting is in the Bergedorf subdivision which is nearly a half hour drive to the southeast from the mother church. The Bergedorf membership is counted as belonging to the mother church in Hamm even though at least half of the approximately forty Bergedorf members seldom attend Christuskirche.

Woldemar Lein came to this church as pastor in 1965. His work takes him to all three locations. On Sunday mornings only the members who can attend services at Christuskirche in Hamm hear him preach. Worship services at Bergedorf are conducted on Sunday afternoons alternately by Pastor Lein, a student pastor or lay minister from the Hamm church.

At Christuskirche a full program of church activities is carried on, including Sunday-School, youth activities, men's and women's work, choral activities, special group meetings, and Wednesday evening prayer and Bible study. A variety of special summer vacation time retreats and camping experiences are carried on for all age groups with considerable enthusiasm.

The church operates a well-organized and well-run weekday kindergarten for approximately fifty children of the community. It is run on a self-sustaining basis, largely on fees paid by parents for the privilege of sending the children to kindergarten while they work in business and industry.

A full-time deaconess, Sister Käte Gammelin, calls on the sick of the congregation and community, helps with the women's work of the parish, and accomplishes what many church-workers find most difficult, the maintaining of a spirit of genuine Christian charity. The membership of Christuskirche in 1967 stood at about 340. In addition a score or more "friends" of the church are regular attenders and supporters, but keep their membership in the State Church. Most of the members are active members. In Germany today, if one wants to be an inactive church member, he tends to remain in the majority State Church because he can there be inactive without loss of prestige among his friends. His church tax is collected automatically and less demand is placed upon him than in one of the evangelical free churches. The result is that Methodist church rolls in Germany contain a relatively high percentage of active members.

The Sanctuary—

In Christuskirche the sanctuary is a masterpiece of beauty and simplicity. On the perfectly laid brick wall at the front of the worship area a huge wooden cross, lit up from behind, is central to the worship area. The cross stands immediately behind the altar which is supported by arched wooden uprights. Two large candles, upheld by giant holders in the shape of the Greek letters Alpha and Omega are set beside an open Bible. The pulpit stands slightly to the right of the altar area from the view point of the congregation. A large wooden slab forming the front of the pulpit has the words "Im Anfang war das Wort" in large letters. To the left, just in front of the listeners are the lectern and the ministers' chairs, perhaps more properly called benches. Slightly to the center and behind the lectern is a large area for ferns, indoor plants, and flower stands, wisely making it possible for the listener to view the beauty of plants and flowers if he so wishes or not to be distracted by them at all if he wishes to keep his attention directed toward the preacher. Finally, the altar-table is surrounded by a semicircular altar step and railing at which communion is served from a common cup.

Pastor Woldemar Lein

The worship area has been described as above not only because it is impressive in itself, but to say that when Pastor Lein ascends the two low steps to the pulpit the congregation expects a ministry of the Word which is appropriate to the setting.

Woldemar Lein conducts much of the opening worship from the center of the platform, several steps below the altar and facing the congregation. His memory for this part of the service seems to be flawless. He supports the congregational singing from his chair by lending his generous vocal effort to the singing, while actually the congregational singing is led by the organ and by the excellent singing of the choir from the rear balcony. The writer was not too favorably impressed by this arrangement because much too often the effectiveness of the singing was hindered by a see-saw effect between congregation and choir. At such times the pastor found it difficult to be a mediator. In spite of these minor crises, the worship service is unusually impressive and significant.

Woldemar Lein reads the scripture, from the pulpit, with considerable intensity but at the same time in a natural expanded speaking tone of voice. Although he is dignified and reserved in his total demeanor, there is nothing still or prepossessing about his bearing. He has a fine sense of humor controlled by a rare instinct for what is fitting and conducive to worship and serious reflection.

He has a sound medium-range speaking voice, but not an exceptionally good one. However, he uses what he has very well excepting on those occasions when he allows the voice to rise in pitch just enough so that it loses some of its natural richness. This, in Pastor Lein, is in no sense a bad fault, for it may actually add some intensity of feeling to what he is saying. The criticism just mentioned was not supported by any mention of it by listeners. It would probably not occur to them to criticize his voice quality. This, of course, also says something about his pleasant acceptable personality.

Pastor Lein is a vigorous man in his early fifties, who, as a young soldier, participated in the ill-fated German march to Rostov in Russia but was fortunate enough to come through the war without physical injury. He occasionally makes use of his wartime experiences in his preaching. One of his parishioners said concerning this, "What I like about our pastor is that he doesn't always talk about the war, like some of the other pastors do."

At the time of the study of his preaching Woldemar Lein was recording secretary of the General Conference of Methodist of the Bundes-republik (West German), and was secretary of the Northwest German yearly conference as well. He does not allow his many activities to prevent him from preparing for the preaching ministry, but concerning this we will let the laymen speak in a succeeding chapter.

He speaks from very scanty notes on one small slip of five by seven inch note-book paper. The listener is hardly ever aware of his notes, because this preacher is continually looking at his congregation as he speaks.

MICHAELIS—Church and Parish

Michaelis holds a position of honor in the minds of the people of Hamburg. When they speak of *Grosse* Michaelis, they mean to say that it is large and grand. However, the name also distinguishes the large Michaelis from Kleine (Little) Michaelis which stands only about a block away from the large church.

The use of Michaelis as the place of meeting for the thousands who come to hear Thielicke preach from its famous pulpit has brought it to the attention of even greater numbers of people. It has not necessarily increased the size of the congregation at Sunday worship services excepting perhaps during the tourist season. At least, no way of measuring the total effect of the Thielicke preaching services on the life of the church has been found. Our

purpose here is not to discuss the effect of
Thielicke's preaching on the church but to
briefly tell the story of the church which serves
as the center for the preaching ministry of Helmut Thielicke.

As early as 1600 a small chapel was built
on the present site to serve as a meeting place
for people who lived outside the walls of the
old city. When the area changed from garden
plots to city lots a large church was needed.
The first Grosse Michaeliskirche was completed in 1669. This large church was hit by
lightning and burned to the ground on March
10, 1750. The present Little Michaelis was
built to serve the congregation during the
planning and building of a large new church.
This Little Michaelis is the church which in
the year 1811 at the demand of the French was
arranged for Roman Catholic worship. Little
Michaelis is located just across the main East-
West Street from the site of the second and
third great St. Michaelis Church. Little Michaelis is prospering today with four crowded
masses every Sunday morning.

The second large St. Michaelis was built by
1762, and the famous tower was completed by
1786 under the supervision and according to
the plan of Ernst Georg Sonnin, whose fame
was considerably increased by its completion.
The people of Hamburg loved this church. It
belonged to the picture of the city and greeted
the seafarer when leaving and returning on the

Elbe River. Built in the form of a cross and upheld by only four giant pillars, so that there is a clear view of the pulpit from every seat, this wonderful baroque church was Sonnin's example of what an evangelical preacher's church should be. After exactly one hundred and thirty years from its completion, in 1906, on a hot July day, Sonnin's masterpiece burned to the ground.

The Hamburg Senate, the entire citizenry, and funds from all over the world supported the rebuilding. Rebuilt according to the famous Sonnin plan, with modern adaptations making it more fire-proof, the present Michaeliskirche was completed and rededicated in 1912. Although seriously damaged in the bombings of World War II, the church was repaired and rededicated in 1947, and the great bells which had been hidden somewhere in the harbor area rang again. The church, as it stands today, with its great balconies, seats 2,550 people.

The high pulpit with its long flight of steps is built of magnificent marble. It is so situated that the preacher can be seen and heard by everyone in the sanctuary. Acoustically Michaelis was so perfectly constructed, that unlike many other great European churches, or American ones for that matter, it is the rival of any theatre in its acoustical characteristics. The altar, also of marble, is twenty meters high. The great altar picture, a glass-mosaic, portrays the resurrection of Christ. Altogether it is, without question, the most richly decorated of the Hamburg churches.

But we must bypass further description of the church, excepting to add that the tower with its great clock visible from all four sides is 433 feet and six inches high from the street level. Leading to a viewing platform 270 feet above the street level is a stairway of 449 steps. The platform, also reached by elevator, is visited by many thousands of people each year because it affords a splendid view of the city and of the great river-harbor only three city blocks away.

Much more might be written about Michaelis as a place of worship with historical significance, perhaps even significant for its own sake. Again, it is significant for our study of the preaching of Thielicke to recall that even with all the architectural, acoustical, and visual advantages, Michaelis does not attract unusually large numbers to its regular services.

The greater Michaelis parish area was inhabited before the war by approximately fifty thousand people. Today, zoned and rebuilt more for business purposes than for dwellings, there are only about sixteen thousand inhabitants, although many more persons work in the area. For this and other reasons, the Sunday morning worship congregation varies in attendance from 150 to possibly 400 at the peak of the tourist season.

Michaelis is accessible to commuters on

main public transportation lines, necessitating only a six to eight minute walk from a near-by station. By automobile it is easily reached from anywhere in Hamburg in less than an hour, and from most subdivisions in thirty minutes or less. The writer's Volvo reached it easily in less than thirty minutes from a northern subdivision.

Dr. Thielicke is not a pastor or even a member of the regular staff of Michaelis. It would therefore be superfluous to describe the inner working of this church. Aside from preaching at Michaelis approximately four times a year, (until 1968), Dr. Thielicke is a member of the Church Board (*Vorstand*). It was said that he seldom finds time to attend the monthly meetings of this board. He was not present in the meeting of the *Vorstand* attended by the writer, nor did he attend the next meeting, for he held a conflicting seminar with theology students which the writer attended.

Religious Characteristics of the Church—

Although the worship services are poorly attended compared to the size of the church, we should not leave the impression that there is little activity in the parish program. One young pastor in Michaelis (there is a head Pastor and three assistant pastors) conducted 128 funerals in 1966, performed numerous wedding ceremonies, conducted the Sunday morning preaching service once a month and several

additional worship services each month, as
for example, a Monday morning communion
service held in the chancel before the great
altar at 8 a.m. each Monday morning. Besides
this he was responsible for a class of catechumens, which, by his own statement, is perhaps
his most challenging task. His greatest opportunity to help people in need and to present
the claims of the Christian faith he finds in
the conduct of the 128 funerals.

The church owns and manages a large fifty-
bed sailors' home, a transients boarding house,
where good clean, economical accommoda-
tions can be found on a temporary basis by any
man who is sober, who may be waiting between
jobs or for some reason is temporarily away
from home. As much as the writer could discover while living in this place for two weeks,
none of these men had attended the church
across the street or had ever heard of Thielicke.
One of the pastors of Michaelis conducts a worship service with these men in the dining room
of the sailors' home on Sunday mornings.

The church has a part-time youth advisor;
and certain youth activities are regularly
scheduled. These activities are largely of a
social and recreational nature. One capable
young woman, when asked about the youth
work of Michaelis, aside from the choral work,
retorted, "What youth work? They call it youth
work, when they sponsor a dance once a month
or keep the ping pong tables full on certain
evenings a week."

As just intimated, the most effective single activity carried on by the church and challenging youth is the training of a large choir under a very capable organist-director. This activity attracts young singers not only from the local parish area, but from all over Hamburg. This choir sings on alternate Sundays in the regular worship service and also sings at the preaching services held in the church by Dr. Thielicke.

All this is reported here only to provide a backdrop, a background, essentially by way of contrast with the interest of the people of Hamburg and of the Michaelis parish area in the preaching of Helmut Thielicke, and also to show that Thielicke, aside from his occasional preaching services, is not directly related as a pastor to the ongoing work of the church.

Thielicke's Use of Michaelis—

Thielicke preaches in the church by invitation and by arrangement with the Church Board. Since the churches belong to the State, he does not pay rent. Special offerings taken up at his preaching services can be used for whatever purpose Thielicke may indicate and not for paying expenses of the meeting. Some money is dropped by his listeners into the regular boxes for offerings; this goes to the regular work of the church. Thielicke uses university students to take up the special offering at his meetings. This writer found the attitude of the ministers and other workers of Michaelis to Thielicke to be friendly, although some of them are somewhat reserved in their praise of his accomplishments.

The Sample Populations

The *random sample of Christuskirche members* (we shall call them Lein listeners) proved to be, proportionately speaking, fairly representative of the geographical distribution of Christuskirche members. Careful study revealed that the 360 members and regularly attending friends of Christuskirche were living in 48 subdivisions and outlying areas of Hamburg and vicinity, giving us ample reason to call Christuskirche a *regional* church. The 55 Lein listeners interviewed were found in 16 subdivisions or outlying areas.

The Sample of Thielicke Listeners—*

The method of developing a list of T Ls and of choosing the sample, already discussed, made it impossible for us to know to what extent the Thielicke sample was representative of the whole body of T Ls. Its reliability was inferred through a comparison with the L L random sample. Geographically the sample represented 18 subdivisions of the city and two outlying areas.

-----

*Hereinafter we shall, in general, follow the practice of using the code-letters: T for Thielicke, T L for Thielicke listener, T Ls for Thielicke listeners, L for Lein, L L for Lein listener, and L Ls for Lein listeners.

Although no determined attempt was made to find T Ls in each subdivision of the city, there is no reason to believe that T Ls could not have been found in all of the subdivisions. Only one pastor of a church, and many were asked, said that he knew of none. Moreover, inquiry of one of the ushers in this church yielded the names of several T Ls. The pastor had only been in his charge for two years; perhaps he was not acquainted with his people. Other pastors invariably knew of a number of T Ls, both in and outside of their congregations. By inference, since there are churches in all subdivisions of the city, there are also people who have heard T in all subdivisions of the city.

Housing—

T and L Listeners for the most part live in apartment complexes. Since most of Hamburg's residential areas are composed of apartments built since the Second World War, the apartments often incorporate group living in a way which leaves families quite independent of each other. In Hamburg the difference between single family living in single family homes and apartment living is often only a very nominal one. For example, apartment dwellers often have small private back and front yards and they are buying and paying for their apartments much as middle-class Americans are buying and paying for their private homes in Boston suburbs. Only nine of the T Ls lived in single family dwellings, and seven or eight persons in the T L sample were found to be living in better than average apartments. None of the interviewees lived in substandard apartments, but a few seemed cramped for space.

Economic Status—

The dwellings of subjects interviewed ran the entire gamut from comparatively low-cost housing to a $50,000 home of a shipbuilder and a high-class, well-furnished apartment of the owner of an import-export business. *Incomes* of T Ls range from that of an incapacitated cook on a small pension to the executive level of salary. Based only on observation and not on exact statistics, we conclude that economically the T listening audience represents all levels of Hamburg income, except the very lowest. A second observation, also unsupported by exact statistics, is that there is no substantial difference between the T and L samples in economic status. Statistically the T sample contained a higher percentage of professional people, such as teachers, ministers, doctors, and dentists. Although doctors and dentists do not become as wealthy in Germany as in America, and among teachers only full professors receive relatively high incomes, we may assume that many persons in the sample enjoy a comfortable standard of living.

Travel Time and Attendance—

The length of time involved in travel to Michaelis, one way, by 82 T Ls is summarized as follows:

(a) 20 persons spend 15 minutes or less,
(b) 33 persons spend from 15 to 30 minutes,
(c) 23 persons spend from 30 minutes to one hour, and
(d) 6 persons spend over an hour.

The average driving time within the city for those who go by automobile is between 17 and 20 minutes, while the average public transportation time is between 35 and 40 minutes—twice as long. The average person interviewed who attends by public transportation has heard T about 8 times, while those who attend by auto have heard him 12 plus times. Perhaps the most striking point derived from a study of travel time is that in the under 15 minute travel classification, none of the subjects who walk to the T preaching services and who live in the adjoining Altstadt and Neustadt districts have heard him more than fifteen times. In the same time category there are five people who come to Michaelis by automobile, who have heard him as many as from 20 to 100 times.

The five persons who have heard T most in our sample have heard him a total of 440 times or a *mean* of 88 times each. Two of these have, according to their own claim, heard him every time he has spoken in Michaelis, which according to the estimate of Dr. Thielicke's very efficient secretary, means that they had heard him 100 times by the end of 1966. One lady, who was converted as a result of Thielicke's preaching, has heard him at Michaelis between 60 and 70 times. Her friends call her a *Thielicke Christian,* even though she has been a Methodist for a decade.

By way of contrast and reflecting the more normal church pattern, the *mode* in attendance for the two and one-half year period of Pastor Lein's ministry in Christuskirche is 125 times. Here the *mean* for persons depending on walking or on public transportation is 85.55, while those who travel to Christuskirche by automobile have a *mean* attendance mark of 70.45. Thus, the L Ls number of times attended is highest by the subjects living in the Hamm subdivision where the church is located, and the attendance of automobile-commuting listeners is more sporadic; in the Thielicke listener sample the reverse was the case. In the community within easy walking distance to to Michaelis no one was found whohad a high record of attendance at T preaching services. Michaelis members with high attendance records invariably were in residence outside the fifteen minute walking distance.

Age and Sex Distribution—

The age and sex distribution of T and L listeners in varying degrees represented the age and sex character of the population of Hamburg. As is well known, two world wars have created a serious imbalance between the number of males and females in certain age

categories. This imbalance may be seen in
Appendix C, p. 315, entitled "The Population
of Hamburg on January 1, 1965, Grouped
According to Age, Sex, and Year of Birth." In
the detailed age and sex profiles, worked out
in our original study of T and L listeners, the
L listener sample most closely resembled
the total population of the city.

To what extent the disproportionately small
number of males appearing in the 36-50 age
group on the Christuskirche profiles and of
both males and females in the T L profile in
the 36-50 age group represents loss of interest
in religion is not known. In interviews with
people of this age group and of other age groups
as well, the opinion was often expressed that
the disillusionment with religion since the war
was greatest in this age group. Certainly, the
heavy loss of lives in the soldier population
of those years strongly affects the present
church membership profiles, for in the age
group of those born between 1915 and 1924
the females outnumber the males approximately 138 to 100.

*Educational Characteristics of T and L
Listeners—*

There is a considerable contrast in the education and training of the two groups of listeners.
Only 12 of the L Ls or 22 per cent have attended
the Gymnasium (university preparatory
school) enroute to their choice of occupations,

while in the T L sample 47 persons or 57 per cent have attended Gymnasium, and 36 of them or 44 percent are either attending the *Universität* or have completed their *Universität* training. Only one Lein listener had completed *Universität* training. Of the L L sample, the majority or 29 have attended the *Volksschule* for their training. To their credit, 12 of these have achieved additional preparation in some form of business or technical work, ranging from secretarial school, handcrafts, or training in trades such as carpentry and mechanical work. Also to their credit, a number of L Ls are Master Craftsmen, having passed the highest tests for craftsmen.

We should note here that the difference in educational level between T and L listeners is greater than the difference in their income levels. Social status is another matter, even in democratic West Germany. Education is one of the evident measures of success in modern Germany as in many other lands. Almost no one has a more respected place than a full professor.

As a full professor, Helmut Thielicke holds a place of honor at Hamburg University and with the knowledgeable people of the city of Hamburg. An interesting related fact is that since the state pays for a university education, the approximately 18,000 university students of Hamburg are privileged people.

The question has often been raised, to what

extent do the listeners with less than an average education understand and appreciate the preaching of Dr. Thielicke? At this point our purpose is only to note several facts that bear on the answer to this question. Among the six T Ls interviewed who had only a *Volksschule* education, all but one had heard Thielicke less than ten times. In fact, four of them had heard Thielicke less than four times. Of those who had *Volksschule* with some added business or technical training there were a number of self-educated people who pride themselves on the books they read and on the fact that they can understand Dr. Thielicke. So there are persons with a meager formal schooling who have heard Thielicke preach many times but most of them are extraordinary people.

Two observations are now evident. Attendance records indicate that the better educated of the sample groups are among the most regular in attendance in both groups of listeners. But it is equally evident that both preachers speak to people with a wide range of education and experiences. Both have strong support from their university-trained listeners, but both also seem to satisfy the needs of the less than average in education person.

Occupational Characteristics—

Here we note one of the sharpest differences between the T Ls and L Ls. Even when clergymen and other religious professionals such as

chaplains, professors of religion, and the editor
of a religious periodical are excluded, the T L
professional group is still more than 9 per cent
larger than the L L professional sample. The L L
groups that outnumber the T L sample groups
are clerical workers, sales workers, craftsmen,
operatives, and housewives.

A relatively large number of ministers were
included in the T L sample, because it was
thought desirable to be able to compare the
ratings by ministers on Ts preaching with that
of laymen. In line with the principle of quota
sampling the T L sample also included 13
professional persons, 14 housewives, a clerical office group numbering 9 persons, a man-
ager-craftsmen-operatives group numbering 10,
and a group of 10 retired and semi-retired persons.

Marital status of Interviewees—

The two groups interviewed closely resembled the distribution indicated by the latest
complete census figures taken from the *Statistical Yearbook* of Hamburg, published in 1967.
There were 1,411,323 persons in Hamburg above
the age of 20. Of this number there were 241,708
single people who had not been married or
approximately 17 per cent. At the same time
there were 49,015 widowers and divorced males
and 193,959 widows and divorcees, accounting
for over 17 per cent of the Hamburg population.
We were therefore not surprised to find un-

usually large numbers of persons in all of these categories in both groups of interviewees, with the exceptions that the number of widows in the Methodist sample was slightly larger percentagewise than in the total population, while the sample included only one divorced person.

We shall complete our description of the two groups of listeners with a brief focus on *church membership, church attendance,* and *offices held.*

Of the 55 L Ls, 50 were members of Christuskirche, two were members of other Methodist churches, and three were in the category of *friends* of the church. The *friends* were actually members of various state churches in the city of Hamburg.

Of the 82 T Ls, 50 were Evangelical Lutherans, 24 were Methodists, and 8 belonged to other denominations and groups. Of the 50 Evangelical Lutherans, 20 were members of Michaelis and 30 were members of other Evangelical Lutheran churches. Of the 24 Methodists, ten are also included in the L L sample, seven others were members of Christuskirche (not in the L L random sample) and the other seven were members of other Methodist Churches.

The eight remaining listeners in the T L sample represent the Evangelical Fellowship (E. U. B.), which has since been united with the Methodist Church, and the Presbyterian, Mennonite, and Roman Catholic Churches. The object-tive was to get a representative sample from Michaelis, from other Lutheran churches, from Christuskirche, from other Methodist groups, and from other denominational groups repre-sented in Hamburg.

For persons in the L L sample, church atten-dance is practically synonymous with having heard Pastor Lein preach but for persons in the T L sample it refers not to how often or how many times they have heard Dr. Thielicke preach but how often or how seldom they go to worship in their own local church or in the church in which they retain their membership.

Without giving the detailed statistical in-formation on church attendance, we simply report the surprising fact that Thielicke lis-teners (excluding university students) made nearly as high a score as Lein listeners on church attendance (Gottesdienst). This un-doubtedly means that the kind of person who chooses to attend Thielicke preaching services, as a rule, takes church attendance to be a mat-ter of importance in his life. Can it be that, in general, the kind of people who go to hear Thielicke are also the people who take seri-ously their obligation to the church to which they belong?

There were a number of notable exceptions to this rule. One T L had not been to her own church for over a year and admitted that she seldom attends any church, but stated that she seldom misses Thielicke's sermons at Michael-is. Another interviewee said, "When I hear the other preachers, they rob me of my faith, but Thielicke gives me back my faith." She also seldom attends the regular worship service.

Another indication of the type of person who attends the Thielicke preaching services was derived from answers to the question: Have you held an office in your church? Forty-two per cent of the T Ls answered *yes*, while only 26 per cent of the L Ls answered *yes*. Offices listed ranged from minister, churchworker, church board member, organist, S S teacher, group leader to group officers. A large number in both groups mentioned participating in choir work. The writer came away with the impression that a great many German Christians had their interest in the church developed through early participation in children's or youth choirs.

The statistics on offices held again supports the impression that Thielicke listeners largely consist of people who are interested in their own churches and are active members in those churches.

Professor Dr. Helmut Thielicke, Th.D.

Chapter 3

HELMUT THIELICKE—THE MAN—
THE PREACHER

Biographical

The account which follows should not be considered a biography. It is, however, a review of some of the significant events and influences which entered into the growth and development of the man whose preaching we are studying.[1]

Helmut Thielicke was born in Barmen, Germany, in early December of 1908. His father was a teacher in a *Gymnasium*. Gymnasium, in Germany, is the designation for a pre-university school. Students who wish to attend a university must attend the Gymnasium rather than a folk-school (*Volksschule)* or a middle-school (*Mittelschule*). His father had a good library and Helmut was afforded all the opportunities available to German children reared in an academic atmosphere.

Barmen is situated in a heavily industrial urban area, north of Bonn and Cologne and south of Dortmund and Essen, called the Wuppertal. This general area of Germany has long been known as an area of cultural and religious ferment and development. Anabaptists, for example, and historians of the Church of the

Brethren look at near-by Krefeld as important
to their beginnings. The people of the Wuppertal have long been known for their piety.

It was in Barmen and the Wuppertal that Helmut Thielicke received his early schooling
from teachers who in later years have received
high commendation from their former student.
The writer visited the site of the Wilhelm-Dörp-
feld-Gymnasium, the school which Thielicke
attended in his teen years in Wuppertal. At the
main entrance of the rebuilt school, for the city
was almost entirely destroyed by the war, one
stands in full view of the great cathedral of the
city on one side of the school, while on the
other side stands the old city hall. Dr. Thielicke
had dedicated *Auf Kanzel und Katheder,* the
book referred to in footnote 1 on page 85, to this
school, thus indicating his appreciation for
the influence of the school on his early development. It would be difficult indeed to measure
the effect of the early training received in the
famous *Gymnasium* in the Wuppertal, which
according to Thielicke had long been known
for its famous successful graduates and its
grand teachers.[2]

Young Helmut was in every way an active,
healthy boy. However, even as a small boy he
was capable of the unusual. In the course of his
sermon entitled "Of the End of All Things,"[3] he
tells how when he was a small boy, his innermost wish was for a ladder-wagon. When he
finally received one and thought that he would

burst for joy, even while his father was carrying it into their home, he broke into tears and cried. But let Thielicke tell it in his own words. "My father scolded me for this sudden howling, accused me of unthankfulness, and later told me what I had answered, namely, 'Sometime it will go to pieces anyway.' "[4] The mature Thielicke interprets his boyhood feelings in the following words: "In the face of a great fulfillment the transitoriness of the beautiful became clear to me; I experienced the shock of finiteness."[5]

Thielicke tells how at the age of fifteen he won a prize on a landscape portrayal entered in a contest sponsored by a Wuppertaler Newspaper. The prize won him a fourteen-day stay in a hotel and vacation place in the Harz mountains. Winning this prize, he admits, went to his head and for a time caused him to think that he possessed some special talent in the area of landscape description. At the time he memorized and imitated the content and style of Walter Flex, the poet of the youth movement of this period. Thielicke undoubtedly did this well enough so that he could pass off the landscape descriptions of this poet as his own while sitting around the campfires with his young companions during the summer wanderings. Eventually these spurious attempts at picturing the landscape became so untruthful and pathetic that they began to disgust young Helmut himself and he soon left the whole thing alone.

Through experiences like these, young Thielicke became aware of the genuine in life and at the same time was immunized against simply copying others or even, as he says, was prevented from becoming simply a member of a school of thought without critically applying his own faculties to an area of belief or thought.

Before he was twenty he worked for a whole year on the problem of tragedy in the German Demetrius dramas and at the time of graduation (*Reifeprüfung*) from the Gymnasium he handed in an opus of over 120 pages as a graduation examination paper. The problem of tragedy still has a place in the cycle of his lectures at the university.

At the time of graduation (*Abitur*) it is required that the student make known his chosen calling. Helmut Thielicke stated that he wished to become a theologian. Whereupon his professor said, "And I suppose you also want to be a pastor?" Thielicke replied promptly, "That I would like to avoid if possible!" Thielicke says that his classmates have reminded him many times of his answer, but that it, nevertheless, accorded exactly with his intentions.[6]

At about the same time Thielicke had the good fortune to attend a conference of churchmen at which Karl Barth participated in a sparkling disputation with certain aggressive Pietists. Thielicke was much impressed by the smoke-blowing theologian who in scintillating argument   interspersed   with   good-natured humor and irony swept away the oppressive steam of the pious self-righteous flesh. As a result young Thielicke's heart was completely won over to theology.[7]

He entered the university of Greifswald at the age of 20, as he says, with unjustified self-confidence. When he was dissatisfied with the small introductory assignments in a class in Old Testament, the old professor, Martin Noth, allowed him to choose his own subject for investigation. Thielicke chose to work on "The Development of Israelite Religiosity from Adam to Christ." The professor accepted the work but explained its deficiency and that without the necessary study tools one must surely come to such a *faux pas*. He also explained what it means to stand before a new beginning with empty hands.

Although the professor had not handled him in an unkindly way, Thielicke fell into a period of doubt acknowledging himself as a complete charlatan. He now found the life to which he had attached himself to be a torment, which in spite of good companions was preventing him from working at the real problems of life. At this juncture of his student life Thielicke became ill. We shall let him tell his own story at some length because of its importance to an understanding of Thielicke as a man.

Now I know, that what was to follow, was a flight into sickness. I had suffered for several years from an enlargement of the thyroid gland, which could have been handled internally with some expectation of results. Even though I was warned by several physicians against the operation, I nevertheless persuaded them with cunning and energy. It was not only the desire for a powerful and quick release, which later also drove me to many a folly, but above everything else it was the desire for once through the pain and depression of spirit, to be led out of the horror vacui and the terrible rudderlessness for which I saw myself paying the price.

Whether he means he was paying the price by being ill or by submitting to an operation is not clear. At any rate, the operation took place and ended catastrophically. Besides a festering and highly life-threatening lung embolism, which made a rib-resection necessary, he became ill with a serious post-operative tetanus which brought him a "deplorable notoriety" in the medical world. For the next four years he wandered from university clinic to university clinic seeking help. In fact, throughout the entire period of study at the university level no one could help him. He says of this period:

Eventually I prolonged my life in a wheelchair, while I continued to work more in despair than in hope. My fellow-students brought me reports on lectures and seminars, which I could hardly attend, and understanding heads of clinics made it possi-

ble for me to arrange a kind of study-room
in the clinics.[9]

Even while his condition was gradually de-
teriorating, he continued to write and study.
He wrote the thesis for his doctor of philosophy
degree on the relation between the *ethical* and
the *aesthetic* during this time. One of the very few
joys of those dark years was experienced when
his book on the subject, beautifully printed,
was presented to him in the clinic. He was not
able to dress himself and had to allow himself
to be brought and driven to his first theological
examination. An "American" hormone, which
cost 1200 marks a month was able to help him
eventually. And later a "German-made" remedy
was found which worked a complete cure.[10]

The medical problem, difficult as it was at
the time is now readily explainable. The very
small "para-thyroid" glands which produce
a hormone preventing tetanus type disease,
were damaged in the operation. A substitute
for this hormone had not been found at the
time of the operation.

In an interview with Dr. Thielicke the writer
commented on his seeming robust health and
boundless energy. The reply was "O, my health
is still a medical problem. I take antitetramia-
cin continuously to be as completely healthy
as I am now." The above facts have been veri-
fied in conversation with a competent medical
practitioner.

Through the suffering and darkness of those years Thielicke came to a new understanding of the meaning of faith. When asked about the meaning of this experience in his life, he said, "My sickness was something *given,* for which I can now be thankful."[11] He writes, "I know now what faith is, and all that was only intellectual that had fascinated me in theology was swept away by completely new impulses."[12]

So it was that during a time of great torment and struggle Thielicke completed his university education at a number of universities, first at Greifswald, and then at Marburg, Erlangen, and Bonn. In 1936 he was called to a professorship at Heidelberg, where he taught until 1940, when he was summarily dismissed because of his criticisms of Nazi policies. During these years he was almost constantly under surveillance by the Nazis. In describing his effort at staying out of the hands of the Nazis he uses the word *Tarnung*, which in English means a kind of *camouflage.* This effort occasionally led him to the point of disgust with himself, when he would feel that one really ought to wash his hands. There were repeated police-searches of his house and *soul-searching* hours with the Gestapo. His dismissal from Heidelberg came shortly after he had openly and sharply protested against the offensive excesses of *Stürmer* publisher Julius Streicher.[13]

At this dismissal Thielicke went to München

to see the Nazi official in charge of university professors and teachers. Here is Thielicke's description of what took place.

> After a very stormy and loud discussion he gave me the following reasons for my dismissal (I wrote down the statement immediately afterwards): As long as there are any faculties of theology left—and it won't be much longer, sir—I shall see to it that only sucking pigs and no wild boars are given professorships. But you belong to the younger generation of theologians who are pugnacious in their cause. These people we can not use. The old ones we'll soon wear down.[14]

A number of officials under the Nazis took it upon themselves to help Thielicke out of his difficulty. One such official used the formula "Thielicke is a National Socialist without knowing it."[15] Several understanding young army officers got him into the army in spite of his former suffering in order to draw away the attention of the Gestapo. Even this experience brought something of value to Thielicke, for it brought him into natural contact with simple and true men from whom one is often isolated. He was released from the army in less than a year.[16]

Doberstein summarizes the next period of Thielicke's life as follows:

> Returning to civilian status in 1941, he

was ordained by Bishop Theophilus Wurm
and became a pastor in Ravensburg, where
he had his first real taste of preaching to a
congregation. During this period he also
made extensive lecture tours throughout
the country until, like Dietrich Bonhoeffer
and other fearless pastors and theologians,
he was forbidden to travel or speak publicly.[17]

During this time when he was virtually interned in his parish, Thielicke completed work
on two books: *Death and Life: Studies in Christian Anthropology,* and *Questions Christianity
Puts to the World: Studies on the Intellectual
and Religious Crisis of the West.* Both manuscripts were smuggled into Switzerland and
were first published only under the name of the
publisher, and only after the war under his own
name.[18]

In 1942 Bishop Wurm called Thielicke to
Stuttgart and achieved a relaxation in the
prohibition against traveling and speaking
and at the same time granted the young man a
generous allowance of time for writing. Let us
turn again to Doberstein's summary of Thielicke's activities during this period.

He was called to Stuttgart where he gave
courses in theology for ministers and delivered popular lectures on Christianity
which week after week attracted crowds of
three thousand and more. This was in the
midst of the bombing of the city by the Allied
forces, and the meetings were moved from

place to place as one auditorium after another was bombed out. After each address several hundreds of volunteer stenographers remained and took down dictated excerpts of the lectures, which they then duplicated privately. Printing was forbidden, but these copies of the Christian message, handed from person to person, found their way to thousands of eager readers.[19]

Thielicke's letters from this time reveal that he believed God was speaking to the people as a result of the events of the war, that theology was becoming more healthy and more central in preaching, and that "all other theology was being buried on the bleak steppes of Russia and under the rubble of the ruins of the homeland."[20]

Near the end of June 1944 Goerdeler, the leader of the German resistance to Hitler, visited Thielicke and asked him to write the section on the new regime's attitude toward Christianity in the proposed revolutionary proclamation of the movement. This he did only three weeks before the catastrophe of the 20th of July in which many of the members of the resistance either perished or endured terrible torture.[21]

During the terrible period of the bombings of Stuttgart and environs Thielicke ministered as best he could to the living. Immediately after the collapse of Germany, he was in the enviable position of being able to serve even the S. S.

troopers in the concentration camps. He took a decisive position against those who wanted to assess a collective guilt on all who had co-operated in any way with the Nazis. He let it be known that he did not see himself as excluded from the community of guilt, and that he was against the collective sentence of condemnation of the former enemies and above all he was against the level at which the judgment was applied. His position was both praised and condemned, depending on who was making the assessment. Some accused him of fostering again the spirit of nationalism, while others blessed him for helping Germans to understand and face their guilt, for freeing the conscience making a genuine repentance possible.[22]

From 1945 to 1954 Thielicke held the chair of systematic theology at Tübingen, and in 1951 and 1952 he also served as rector of the university. During this time he carried on a heavy correspondence, published books on dogmatics, theology, nihilism, and did the major part of the work on his *Theological Ethics,* Vol I, 1951, and Vol. II, 1955.

When in 1954 Thielicke received the call to become the first dean of the newly established faculty of theology at the University of Hamburg, he was conscientiously unable to avoid acceptance of the challenge this position presented him. So, although some of his best friends felt that for him to leave Tubingen, an old and firmly established theological institution with a large student-body from all parts of Germany and the world, would be to commit the greatest folly of his life, he saw no other possibility than to understand the call to Hamburg as the direction of a higher hand.[23]

In his position as professor and dean he helped to select a strong faculty and build a strong library. From 90 students in the first year the student body grew to 260 by the fall of 1956. During these years Thielicke continued his writing and preaching. He undertook a preaching mission in East Germany (DDR), which was not accomplished without difficulty. Since that time he has been unable to obtain visas to enter the Zone for preaching, but has driven through the Zone to West Berlin or flown in by air.

His first visit to America was made in 1956, following invitations from Chicago Theological Seminary and several other institutions to deliver lectures. There is no necessity here to review this journey or his many other journeys to various parts of the world, excepting to say that he was always writing and preaching, and as a result has published a number of books recounting his experiences abroad and his reflections on these experiences. These will be discussed briefly in the chapter on "Helmut Thielicke as a Writer."

Helmut Thielicke—Preaching in Michaelis

In his letter to his friends at the end of 1954 Thielicke wrote, "That I now have the possibility of preaching regularly in St. Jacobi, helps me not to forget the essential themes of the theological ministry and to remain tied to what is significant.[24]

In a Christmas letter one year later he explained that the spiritual shaft of his Hamburg existence is set forth once a month in the sermons at Michaelis.[25] He explains that it was because of the crowds that "they" had to give up the smaller church (St. Jacobi). In the same letter he tells about meeting listeners who had never before been in a church, who had not been baptized nor instructed in the faith.

In the same letter he speaks of receiving many letters from listeners, and of the problems which weigh on his mind resulting from the responsibilities inherent in a ministry to so many people. He even adds that he has sometimes considered whether he should not go entirely into a preaching ministry.[26]

He lists the names of numerous secular groups to whom he has spoken and how this necessitates making adjustments to the climate and general situation of the group. He repeatedly writes that the spiritual shaft of his preaching is developed in his monthly sermons at Michaelis.

All of the entries concerning his preaching

ministry at Michaelis show a deep concern for the people who come to hear him.[27] In a 1956 letter he says he is fortunate to experience a liturgy at Michaelis which in its simplicity gives something to the large number of people who are strange or foreign to the church. It is known that Thielicke was for some years not permitted to conduct the liturgical part of the service, and when permission was given it was not achieved without a struggle. Some concessions were made of necessity. For example, permission was given for the organist to play for an hour before the service began while the people waited inside the church rather than outside.

Concerning the nature of the preaching and the principles of preaching which are evident in the ministry of Dr. Thielicke in Michaelis an account will be found in Chapter 5.

During the first years in Hamburg, Thielicke held two preaching services per month, on Saturday evening and on the following Sunday morning. With what regularity is not clear. A precise record of those years was not made available to the writer. In a 1959 letter Thielicke wrote, "of my own free will I have had to again give up the Saturday-Sunday pattern of services, because it finally was beyond my powers to continue."[28] He had just completed the series on "How the World Began," which had lasted two and one half years. It must be noted that the series was interrupted for journeys abroad and for summer vacation periods.

One of the side-lights on the preaching services in Hamburg is the fact that the *offerings* taken up were used for various projects initiated by Thielicke, such as for the sending of books to the East Zone of Germany. He wrote, "My Michaelis congregation has offered large sums for that purpose."[29]

The task of continuing the preaching eventually became too much of a burden, together with all his other duties, so that he had to diminish the number of services. To allow the quality of his messages to deteriorate, he could not tolerate. In 1962 he wrote: "In spite of my thankfulness, I must say freely that in a comparative sense, nothing has given me so much desperate labor as the preaching in Michaelis." An American would probably have said, "Nothing has cost me so much painful work."

We are not surprised therefore that the number of Saturday evening preaching services was cut down to not more than four a year. The number of services diminished gradually from once a month to four times a year during 1964 and 1965.

Exactly when and how this occurred is not clear from the record, but four one-hour sermons in Michaelis has been the standard during the last two years at least. Meanwhile, the great church auditorium continues to be packed to capacity, even though it is no longer necessary to come an hour or more early to be sure of a seat.

It is clear that Helmut Thielicke had preached at Michaelis at least a hundred times by the end of 1966.

NOTES AND REFERENCES

[1]Some of the material for this chapter was derived from interviews with Dr. Thielicke but for the most part the writer has been forced to rely on his own translation of the book by Dr. Thielicke, entitled: *Helmut Thielicke—Auf Kanzel und Katheder,* published by Furche-Verlag H. Rennebach K. G., of Hamburg, Germany, in 1965. Translated the title reads *Helmut Thielicke at Pulpit and Rostrum.* Thielicke makes a point to remind the reader that the book is not to be considered a biography. It is a partial account of significant events in the life of the author, who himself looks on the book as a work report. Actually, the major part of the book is made up of letters written by Thielicke to his friends and fellow-workers. The letters written at various stages of his life are chronologically arranged.

[2]Helmut Thielicke, *Auf Kanzel und Katheder,* p. 10. (See footnote 1 above.) Hereinafter this book by Helmut Thielicke will be referred to in citations as K & K.

[3]Helmut Thielicke, *Wie modern darf die Theologie sein?* (Trans. M. D.) (Stuttgart: Quell-Verlag,

1967), p. 77. (The writer heard the sermon referred to in St. Michaelis, on February 11, 1967.)

[4]*Ibid.,* p. 77.

[5]*Ibid.*

[6]K & K, p. 12.

[7]K & K, p. 12.

[8]K & K, p. 13.

[9]K & K, p. 14.

[10]K & K, p. 15.

[11]In an interview on June 15, 1967.

[12]K & K, p. 15.

[13]K & K, p. 23.

[14]K & K, pp. 23-24.

[15]K & K, p. 24.

[16]K & K, p. 25.

[17]Helmut Thielicke, *The Waiting Father* (New York: Harper and Row, Publishers, 1959), p. 9. See translator's introduction by John W. Doberstein.

[18]K & K, p. 26.

[19]H. T., *The Waiting Father, op. cit.,* translator's introduction, p. 9.

[20]K & K, p. 42.

[21]K & K, pp. 44-45.

[22]K & K, p. 56.

[23]K & K, p. 57.

[24]K & K, p. 66.

[25]K & K, p. 68.

[26]K & K, pp. 76-77.

[27]K & K, p. 131.

[28]K & K, p. 173.

[29]K & K, p. 183.

Chapter 4

HELMUT THIELICKE—THE WRITER

Since he was twenty years of age, there has scarcely been a period of more than a few months when Helmut Thielicke was not writing something with a view to its eventual publication. From reading his letters to his friends as published in *Auf Kanzel und Katheder,* from reading his numerous writings and sermons—if we may make this distinction between his sermons and other writings—and from conversation with him, it is evident that he is constantly, and has been since his early years in various universities, planning to write or writing, and planning to preach or preaching. He is continually investigating, searching, immersing himself in the material necessary to the mastery of a problem, a theme or a sermon subject; with the intention of writing, delivering, and usually of publishing the results, that is, if he considers the material worthy of publication. As a general rule he works on a subject only if he expects the result of his work on that subject to be worth publishing when completed.

For Thielicke to prepare a sermon means to write that sermon before it is preached. As a matter of fact most of his published sermons are simply the sermons as written before delivery, edited and corrected for publication. Also, our study shows that his sermons must be considered a substantial part of his writings even though for convenience sake we will make a distinction between sermons and other writings.

The *purpose* of this chapter is to review the writings of Helmut Thielicke and to relate these writings to his preaching ministry. This will be done chronologically, according to the order of publication in the German language.

In the review of the writings by Dr. Thielicke which follows, the reader is asked to turn to the Bibliography on Page 317 for the facts of publication not given in the text, especially for the place of publication and the names of publishers. In the text we shall first make mention of a book by its German title and then give its English equivalent in parentheses.[1] In any subsequent mention of the book we may use either the German or the English title, whichever promises to be the more useful.[2]

Thielicke's Early Writings

In his early books Thielicke struggles with the problems that concern the serious young student of theology and of ethics. Even the material he covered in his early studies continually finds its way into his preaching and teaching.[3]

Thielicke's two earliest books, written, as we have mentioned in Chapter 3, while he was a university student, were undoubtedly, of all his writings least related to his ministry as a preacher. His first book, *Das Verhaltnis swischen dem Ethischen und dem Asthetischen: eine systematische Untersuchung,* (The Relationship Between the Ethical and the Aesthetic; a Systematic Investigation), 1933, gives indication of what is to be a major interest of Thielicke throughout his life, that is the interest in the relation between the ethical and other elements of life, whether aesthetic, religious, or more specifically theological.

Geschichte und Existenz: Grundlegung einer evangelischen Geschichtstheologie, (History and Existence: Foundation for a Protestant Theology and History), 1935, is a book in which Thielicke concerned himself with the problem of the relation of the vertical dimension of revelation to the horizontal areas of life in which we as Protestants find ourselves, including the laws of the state, the prevailing culture, and in personal life. In *Kanzel und Katheder,*[4] Thielicke explains that in this book as in others, he was not interested in political, commercial, or cultural matters for their own sake, but is interested in how man sees himself in relation to these areas of life. A second great interest in this book is what happens in a man and especially to his forms of expression, when he finds God and thereby finds himself as well.

Fragen des Christentums an die moderne Welt; eine christliche Kulturkritik (Christianity's Questions to the Modern World; a Christian Critique of Culture) was begun in 1941. Part of Thielicke's work on this book was done during the time when he was virtually interned, when his travel and preaching were curtailed. The manuscript was smuggled across the Swiss border and was finally published at Geneva in 1945. In 1947 it was also published in Germany and made available to Germans. It was read widely in the concentration camps by former Nazis detained by the Allies. Thielicke writes that in this book he was attempting to answer some of the grave problems raised by the development of the Nazi regime in Germany. He was trying to find answers for himself as much as for others. In a letter he writes of this book as follows:

> It is to be a comprehensive view of secularization, which engulfs the individual areas of culture, and which on the whole is to contain something of an anthropology of secular man. Here, for example, are some of the chapter headings: . . . Conflict and Adventure, Christ and the Technical Age, Psychotherapy and the Care of Souls (Pastoral Care), and The Reality of the Demonic.[5]

Another book on which Thielicke worked intermittently between 1939 and 1945 was *Tod und Leben: Studien zur christlichen Anthropologie* (Death and Life, Studies toward a Christian Anthropology), which was also smuggled into Switzerland for publication.[6]

In this book Thielicke struggled with the facts of life and death in the context of wartime death and destruction. His writing of this book is an example of his dealing with the most pressing issues as they arise.

It was during this time that Thielicke discovered his words could reach the ear and heart of the people. He writes:

> I experienced what I did not know, that the gospel could help and comfort, and that at death-beds and in the quarters of those who had received death notices from the battlefields, it could accomplish what I had not even allowed myself to dream that it could do.[7]

From this time on, in his preaching, Thielicke is never to be unaware of the fact of suffering and death.

Post-War Sermons and Other Writings

In 1947 Thielicke wrote his book dealing with the problem of the German Church in its readaptation to its task in post-war Germany, under the title *Kirche und Öffentlichkeit; zur Grundlegung einer luterischen Kulturethik* . . . Church and Public Life: Toward Establishing a Lutheran Cultural Ethic . . .)[8] Thielicke's writing of this book is another example of his practice of dealing with the most pressing issues as they arise.

An important book of sermons not published until 1949, but which represented several years of work during the most difficult part of the war, was published under the title *Der Glaube der Christenheit; unsere Welt vor Jesus Christus* (The Faith of Christendom; Our World Before Jesus Christ). In several places Thielicke calls this a *Laiendogmatik* (A book of doctrine for laymen). During the war, when these sermons were preached, the throng of listeners moved from one bombed out church to another, until no churches were left in Stuttgart. At one point in this series Thielicke preached eight times in succession on one commandment, "Thou Shalt Not Kill."[9]

A volume in English consisting of Chapters 18 to 32 out of this *Laiendogmatik* has been published under the title, *Man in God's World*, 1963. A chapter out of *Fragen des Christentums*, is included as Chapter XII in this volume. Chapter XII is entitled "The Reality of the Demonic." Thielicke's great concern in these sermons is to answer the persistent questions raised about belief in the face of wartime conditions, as well as in the face of the scientific revolution.

In one of his brief internal summaries in the chapter on "The Reality of the Demonic," he says, "We have had to conclude again and again that the reality of the demonic is not simply a principle but a real and personal power."[10]

In our study we are interested in determining whether this belief in the reality of the demonic comes through to his listeners in more recent years.[11] Perhaps the dominant purpose of the series in this book is the desire to help modern men, and especially the youth of the time, to come to a living faith, a faith in which there is at the same time an acceptance of the great mass of new knowledge through science. Some of the chapter titles are as follows: Man in the Cosmos, Creation and Cosmology, The World View of Biology, The Origin of Man, The Biblical Message of Miracles, Free Will and Predestination.

Another book which was not available for study to the writer was *Theologie der Anfechtung . . .* (Theology of Temptation) published in 1949, at Tubingen. This book was written in defense of theology during the same years when Thielicke was putting a major amount of time into his *Theological Ethics*. Thielicke cites this book as profitable reading on the meaning of dogmatics and on why it is studied.[12]

Der Nihilismus; Entstehung, Wesen und Uberwindung, 1950, (published in English as *Nihilism, Its Origin and Nature—with a Christian Answer,* 1961) was first of all a series of lectures by Thielicke to his students at Tubingen, delivered to them in the largest hall of the University and to students in overflow rooms nearby. This book reflects the widespread feeling of hopelessness and despair of the

post-war years, a despair that too often issued
into a feeling that those who were attempting
to incite interest in democracy or for that matter to revive loyalty to old forms of religion,
were merely on a new road to frustration and
deception. Nihilism, the idea that ultimately
Nothingness prevails and that the world is
meaningless was a real danger to German
youth. Thielicke attacks this philosophy and
this tendency with everything at his command.
He describes the breakdown that occurs when
the Christian view of man is lost,[13] and how
separation of the world from its absolute relation to God, leads to the destruction of the self.[14]

In presenting the positive side of the Christian gospel as an answer to man's needs, Thielicke says:

> Perhaps it has been unfortunate that gener-
> ally the churches have been too one-sided
> in seeing Christ only in connection with the
> overcoming of guilt, with forgiveness and
> justification. This is, of course, the most
> important thing. But just because the world
> problem revolves around sin and grace, the
> total existence of the world is essentially
> affected.[15]

The Christian faith must be seen in its relationship to the whole round of life. One must
not separate the earthquake of original sin
from its symptoms and sequelae, the rifts,
fissures and convulsions in the world-struc-
ture, but must rather keep in view the totality

of the disaster. Thielicke constantly reminds his audiences that the New Testament speaks of suffering and death. In Christ we have a figure in whom the powers of guilt, suffering, and death are overcome, or better yet, says Thielicke, through Christ they are robbed of their power to separate, so that they are no longer able to cut off contact with God. By holding on to him we are at the breach, holding the hand of the Father.[16]

When Thielicke lectures to his students there are times when he becomes not only an apologist for the Christian faith, but an evangelist. This is as true today as in the days following the war. Behind the man with the scholarly approach there is the man with a warm personal faith. He is certain that the "one and only thing that counts is that there should exist a company of people who are ready to be bound again by that ultimate tie which was lost and then live their lives vicariously and consciously as men who have been blessed and redeemed in the midst of panic."[17]

The three-volume *Theologische Ethik, (The Theological Ethics),* represents Thielicke's greatest literary effort to date; at least twenty years of work and deep concern went into the effort. This is no mean accomplishment for a man engaged in an otherwise crowded schedule. Vacation periods were often set aside for unmolested work on the *Ethik.* It was a great disappointment for Thielicke that the work of translating the *Ethik* into English was accomplished so slowly, and as a result, he writes that it was a cause for regret that many American students and theologians often knew him only through the published sermons.[18]

The three-volume work, published at various times between 1951 and 1964 in Germany, is well on its way to being used by European students as a standard work on theological ethics. As such it fills a long-existing need. Our research indicates that these books are not read, as we say, from cover to cover, but as other standard theological works, they are used as a reference source. The question in our test instrument concerning the reading of books by Dr. Thielicke elicited the following information regarding the reading of the *Ethik:* 17 of the 82 T Ls had read at least "a little" or "a part" of at least one of the volumes.[19] Of eight ministers in the sample, four had read the *Ethik.* Two ministers had read it more extensively than any of the other persons claiming to have read the work. Seven readers of the *Ethik* were students, all but one representing the advanced theology student group. The rest of the 17 included two teachers, one editor, one doctor of economics, one medical doctor, and one merchant. The latter, along with 12 of the 17, admitted that he had read only "a little" of the volume. Several said they had read only the part on sex ethics. From this information one could conclude that for the most part the *Ethik* will serve the needs of ministers and ministerial students.

Table 2

EIGHTY-TWO THIELICKE LISTENERS REPORT
ON THEIR READING OF BOOKS BY THIELICKE

Readers	German Title	English Title
41	Das Bilderbuch Gottes	The Waiting Father
30	Vom Schiff aus gesehen	Voyage to the Far East
19	Das Gebet (Vater Unser)	Our Heavenly Father
17	Ethik	The Theological Ethics
11	Leiden an der Kirche	The Trouble with the Church
10	In Amerika ist alles anders	(In America Everything Is Different)[20]
9	Das Leben kann noch einmal beginnen	Life Can Begin Again
8	Wie die Welt begann	How the World Began
7	Zwischen Gott und Satan	Between God and Satan
7	Zwischen Himmel und Erde	Between Heaven and Earth
6	Auf Kanzel und Katheder	(At Pulpit and Rostrum)
5	Die Lebensangst	Out of the Depths The Silence of God
4	Der Dinzelne und der Apparat	(The Individual and the Machine)
4	An die Deutschen: Rede zum 17. Juni	(An Address to the Germans: on the 17th of June)
2	Theologie der Anfechtung	(A Theology of Temptation)
2	Glaube der Christenheit	Man in God's World
2	Was heisst Freiheit?	The Freedom of the Christian Man
2	Von der Freiheit ein	(The Freedom to be Human)

2 Ich glaube	(I Believe)
2 Fragen des Christentums an die moderne Welt	(Christianity's Questions to the Modern World)
2 Zur Entmythologisierung	(Concerning Demythologizing)
2 Das Schweigen Gottes	(The Silence of God)[21]

Source: Lay Expectation Factor Study, 1968. M. Dirks, B.U.S.T.

In this account we are more interested in the relation between the writing of the *Theological Ethics* and the preaching of Thielicke than in a content description of the work. Our interviews indicated that the ministers, professors and knowledgeable friends of Dr. Thielicke believe that the writing of the *Ethics* has had a salutary effect on his preaching over the last twenty years. Perhaps more important for this study is Thielicke's own view of the relation of his work on the *Ethics* to preaching. In his book, *The Trouble with the Church*,[22] in relation to his discussion of *Docetism* in preaching, he writes:

> Actually I wrote the Ethics in order to do the theological background work for preaching. I attempted to interpret what man is in his worldly reality and thus to explore the various areas of his existence: I sought to catch the law and the gospel, judgment and grace, in the particular refraction that resulted when the divine light fell upon the many-sided prism of human existence.[23]

In this paragraph we have his expression of his reason for writing the *Ethics* and his condensed description of what he attempted to do in the writing of the larger work. Thielicke goes on to explain that only in this way did he feel the he could find his way out of *Docetism.* On the same page he concludes: "Thus the work on the *Ethics* helped me to preach." Even though he comments that readers and listeners hardly ever saw the inner relationship between his two areas of work—the preaching and the work on the Ethics—that connection was none the less effective in determining the character of his work in both areas.

The fact that Thielicke took upon himself in the *Ethik* to be very thorough in his study and to avoid the easy answer at all times has undoubtedly had an effect on his preaching through the years. The impression that in the *Ethik* he sometimes becomes wordy in his attempt to bring about clarity is attested to even by German scholars, who are accustomed to the more tedious and lengthy explanations of their continental colleagues. However, this characteristic, if it is a characteristic of the *Ethik,* does not become a part of Thielicke's sermon style. On the other hand, his masterful use of language is in evidence in the *Ethik* as it is in his sermons and lectures.

When asked how he has time for so much studying and writing Thielicke explained that the immense amount of work expended on the

Ethik had caused him to curtail his preaching and his other activities to a considerable extent. It is significant that it did not, however, prevent him from concurrently writing, delivering, and publishing most of the writings we have already briefly reviewed. These include many of his most significant volumes of sermons, lectures and theological works. It should be added that there is a great deal of written material, published and unpublished, that is not included in this study. As intimated earlier, the work on the *Ethik* and the work on the larger *Dogmatik* has provided a wealth of material for preaching.

For our present purpose, perhaps the most important point that needs to be made is that Thielicke takes special pains to do in his preaching what he has done in *The Ethics,* in the larger work, and in his later book, *The Ethics of Sex,* that is, he tackles difficult and ticklish problems in the relationship of individuals to each other, to institutions, and to government, and seeks to apply theological-ethical guidelines, without simply making easy pronouncements.

The main thrust of *Die evangelische Kirche und die Politik; ethisch-politischer Traktat über einige Zeitfragen* . . . (The Protestant Church and Politics; Ethico-Political Tractate About a Few Problems of Our Time . . .), 1953, is based on the premise that one dare not preach as if there were no great questions to be faced in his time. The church stands over the questions of the time. It is not enough for the church to foster individual piety, but she must help the people with real problems in their everyday living.[24]

At the time this book was written the foremost questions facing the German people were the question of rearmament, the question of how best to foster reunification of Germany, and what position to take in the cold war.[25] Thielicke took a mediating position. He faced the problems of the struggle between the labor unions and management in the same way. He concludes that the church, as such, has no final official word to say, but the Christian in his position as a voter or as a representative functionary on one side or the other has to be helped to see how a "modus-convivendi" can be found, and how, within the context of government or business, it can be decided upon.

This general approach to current problems has often brought Thielicke criticism from representatives of one or the other or of both sides in a conflict, but it has left him free to speak and to minister to members of both sides. In this study we shall forego the task of spelling out how, according to Thielicke, the minister or the layman is to go about his task in this respect. However, this is what Thielicke undertakes to do in this book.

He clearly advocates that the church has to say a decisive "no" to totalitarianism of either right or left. He criticized Karl Barth for speaking of a "socially constructive idea" in relation to communist Hungary.[26] Thielicke's position on communism has made him *persona non grata* in the East Zone of Germany, whereas some other German churchmen are permitted on occasion, with proper permission, to go to the East Zone.

In general, Thielicke is opposed to the idea that church groups through their official representatives should take official positions and make official pronouncements on the problems of the day. But when asked in an interview by the writer about the criticism from certain ministers that he refuses to take a clear position on some issues, he replied, "It just isn't so; no one has taken a position so often and on so many issues as I have. Of course, I am sometimes asked to take a position on issues where it would be both foolish and useless to do so. Then I must decline . . . or wait for the right opportunity." He believes that one must guard his opinions carefully and must earn the right to speak out by diligent research and careful preparation. Moreover, as indicated in the book we are discussing, he is careful to maintain the reputation of the church, for how shall she influence men who have lost their respect for her ministers.

Das Gebet, das die Welt umspannt; Reden über das Vater Unser, (The Prayer that Encircles the world; Discourses on the Lord's Prayer), is composed of sermons delivered to congregations in Stuttgart during the last years of the war and into the period of total military and political collapse and during the beginning of the occupation. Although first published in German in 1953, the series did not appear in its English translation until 1960. Next to *Das Bilderbuch Gottes* and the travel-book entitled *Vom Schiff aus gesehen,* which we will discuss briefly in this chapter, *Das Gebet* was read by more of the 82 T Ls of our study than any other Thielicke writing.[27]

In his introduction to the book Thielicke himself says there was not a single question that could not have been brought to the Lord's Prayer, and not a one that would not have been suddenly transformed if it were put in the form of a prayer. Thielicke demonstrates that the Lord's Prayer is truly the prayer that spans the world. In the course of the series Thielicke used each short phrase of the prayer as a text for at least one sermon. He spoke in two parts (twice) on "Our Father Who Art in Heaven," and in two parts on "Forgive Us Our Debts."

Perhaps this double emphasis on these two phrases says something important to us not only about the Lord's Prayer, but incidently, also about the man we are studying. What are his points of emphasis in these messages? First, Thielicke stresses that we can deal with our fear that God does not exist only when we realize that God has called first to us, and only

if God has first spoken to us in Jesus. Times of
suffering and terror become times of visitation
when we realize that it is Jesus Christ who
teaches us to pray "Our Father."

In part two he stresses that the main thing
is not the petitions we utter, but that we enter
into communion with God. Then we can know
that we have a shepherd in Jesus and that we
have a Father. Thielicke also lays great stress
on the corporateness of the prayer—"Our
Father." "We are young and old, rich and poor,
learned and simple; we belong to all races and
ages on earth."[28] He tries to tie German believers together with believers in all lands,
even in the time of their great isolation and
defeat.

In part one of "Forgive Us Our Debts," after
describing the awful accumulated guilt, the
lack of love, and the suffering in which *we* are
all involved, Thielicke shows his listeners how
only Christ can help *us* (he always includes
himself) with the accumulated guilt, the lack
of love, and the suffering in which we are involved. "He helps us by letting us see his loving
and sympathetic understanding, in other words,
by letting us see his Cross."[29]

In part two of this sermon we are led to see
how Christ helps us through his forgiveness.
Incidently, part two of "Forgive Us Our Debts"
was the last sermon delivered by Thielicke
before the occupation of Stuttgart. Thielicke
took the occasion to say in effect, that when

men are saying, let us find and punish the
guilty parties, I must rather find and be sure
of my own forgiveness. He goes on to stress
that the world lives by the few righteous in
Sodom. The world lives by the uplifted hands
of Christians. He asks the question: how can
the dreadful law of retaliation ever be broken?
His answer, in part, is found in the following
paragraph:

> . . . forgiveness provides the sole possi-
> bility of the world's ever escaping the law
> of the echo, that dreadful, chaotic law by
> which nations and individuals are constant-
> ly inflaming and provoking one another be-
> cause of the "other's fault," and swelling the
> avalanche of guilt and retribution to ever
> more gigantic proportions.[30]

Thus Thielicke's appeal, while on the one
hand intensely personal, takes cognizance of
corporate aspects of guilt and forgiveness.

In 1954 a book of sermons entitled *Die Lebensangst und ihre Überwindung,* (Life's Deepest
Fear and Its Solution), was published. These
sermons were also preached between 1942 and
1951 to people living in fear of death, in anxiety,
and in guilt, arising in an age of evacuations,
mass bombing, and mass burials. The word
solution, used above in the translation is hardly
an adequate word for *Überwindung.* More exactly it has the meaning of overcoming and
surmounting. This was the task of evangelical
ministers in those years, helping their listen-

ers to overcome and to surmount their fears.

Two small volumes of sermons taken from *Lebensangst* have been published in English. *Out of the Depths,* in 1962, includes a selection of nine sermons with the following titles: The God of Ends, On Death, Between the Horsemen of the Apocalypse, Theology in the Face of Death, In the Depths, The Question Concerning the Gracious God, Jesus' Conversation with Nicodemus by Night, Son of God or Brother Man, World History and World Judgment. Analysis of these titles and the sermons themselves illustrates how Thielicke seems to understand the plight of men alone in their guilt or in their fear of death, and how he raises the questions they raise, such as *where was God when* . . . ? and many others. They reveal how he brings the gospel to bear on the situation in which men find themselves, so that they are able to find new hope in some great biblical affirmation.

The second volume is named *The Silence of God,* which is also the title of the second sermon in the collection. The background and the basic themes are the same as in *Out of the Depths.* As one minister expressed it in conversation with the writer of this study, "Thielicke repeats the same theme over and over again— the theme of the lost son, the gracious father, and the joy of forgiveness with its possibility of the renewal of life." To be sure, the parable of the lost son is not mentioned, but the meaning is there, in the sermons of this book and of many of the others. Part II of this book is composed of Festival Sermons on the great themes of Christmas, Good Friday, Easter, and Whitsunday. Here is hope; God is not *only* silent.

Zwischen Gott und Satan; die Versuchung Jesu und die Versuchlichkeit des Menschen, (Between God and Satan), first appeared in 1938, in the crucial time for the church in Germany. Thielicke himself says that it was intended to strengthen the followers of Jesus Christ in their resistance to ideological tyranny. It was reissued in 1946, and again in 1955. The English version was published in 1958, a translation of the 1955 form of the book. The entire book of 77 pages is written in four chapters, each with from 8 to 13 short one- to three-page sections appropriate for daily or consecutive reading. The book centers, as the German title indicates, on the temptations of Jesus and the "temptability" of men. Every short section ends with a positive, helpful, or thought provoking statement. The figure of Satan is as real in the mind of the author at the time of the latest publication of the book as at its first appearance in 1938. Our flat prose in no way does justice to Thielicke's presentation of Jesus, as for example on the last full page of the book in the following words: "Sinless and yet tempted—that is, as we see now, a riddle which our intellect will never grasp—a marvel before our eyes, a divine profundity, like all that meets us in Jesus." The presence of Jesus is real to Thielicke when in closing the book he writes, "And it is the peace given by the other certainty, that even in that event (the event of our temptation), and even in those depths Christ is with us." Typical of the Christology espoused by Thielicke is the phrase *Jesus our Lord and brother!*

By far the best-known book by Dr. Thielicke is *Das Bilderbuch Gottes; Reden über die Gleichnisse Jesu,* (God's Picture-book; Discourses on Jesus' Parables), first published in 1957. In English it is published under the title, *The Waiting Father,* as translated by John W. Doberstein, who has been most effective as translator of Thielicke's works. He was able to put into English much of the original flavor and intention of the German words.

Why is *Das Bilderbuch Gottes* the best-known of Thielicke's writings? The fact that it has a stimulating title which is easily remembered and evokes its own response even before one sees the name of the author, the fact that it centers on the parables (*Gleichnisse*) of Jesus, together with the fact that its messages are easily comprehended by the whole range of listeners and readers—these are all contributing factors. When the series was delivered it provoked a most favorable response because Thielicke is at his best in preaching on the parables. A combination of depth of understanding of the needs of people and the ability of Thielicke to use vivid word pictures help to make the listener feel the contemporary relevance of the parables. These are perhaps some of the important factors in achieving the success reached by the preacher in this series of sermons. To explain more completely how this is done demands a detailed examination of one or more of these sermons. In Chapter 6 a sermon analysis will be attempted.

Offenbarung, Vernunft und Existenz; Studien zur Religionsphilosophie Lessings . . . (Revelation, Reason, and Existence; Studies in Lessing's Philosophy of Religion . . .), 1957, was published as the result of a long-standing interest in Lessing's philosophical works. In 1936, at the age of 28, Thielicke had published his first book entitled *Vernunft und Offenbarung,* (Reason and Revelation), on his confrontation with Lessing. We list this book here, not to discuss it, but to indicate Thielicke's breadth of scholarly interest. It is a book for scholars. None of the 82 T Ls remembered reading it, though if each had been asked specifically about the book, it is possible that one or more of the ministers or scholars might have known the book. Thielicke looks at Lessing as having anticipated Kierkigaard in his understanding of *truth.* In general he says that to discuss Lessing is to carry on an argument with him. In his conclusion he says one must remember that "basically, in the final analysis, Lessing is not a preacher and not a teacher, and is really not a speculative philosopher, but he is an exercise-master, who is concerned with intellectual-spiritual training, in which the truth must come to light."[31] It was writings such as this book which made Thielicke's friends wonder whether he would ever be able to speak to the common man.[32]

The significant point here is that this book represents the kind of scholarship which allows Thielicke to quote from the great German writers, poets, thinkers, philosophers, historians and theologians. The list of names of writers he quotes from is simply too extensive to be included here. His extensive personal library is not just decoration for his two large studies, the one in his home and the other at the university.

A little 41 page booklet that has gone through a number of printings in both German and English is entitled *Kleines Exerzitium für Theologen,* 1959, (A Little Exercise for Young Theologians, 1962). Some of the highlights of this book are reported here, because they are typical of Thielicke's attitude as a preacher. First, Thielicke calls for theologians and preachers, whether young or old to be responsible both toward the intellectual task and to the community. Secondly, in a very forthright section aimed at young theologs his main purpose is to get them to "maintain a lively—

even theological—dialogue with the ordinary children of God."[33]

He tries to set dogmatics into its proper perspective as a systematic discipline, in which the attempt should be made to include the whole of the study of revelation and to assign its details to their proper place in the whole.[34] This is the only way to avoid sectarian heresy. It might be noted in this connection that Thielicke has the ability to speak to listeners of widely different religious backgrounds, both Protestant and Catholic.

Typical of Thielicke's teaching and pertinent for preaching is his warning against increasingly thinking and speaking of God in the third person instead of in the second person, so that, as he says, "I can no longer read the word of Holy Scripture as a word to me, but only as the object of exegetical endeavors."[35]

A statement on theological method is pertinent to our discussion of *confrontation with decision.* Thielicke says:

> Essentially, theological method is characterized by the fact that it takes into account that God has spoken, and that now what God has spoken is to be understood and answered. But it can only be understood when I (1) recognize that what has been said is directed to me, and (2) become involved in formulating a reply. Only out of this dialogue is the theological method comprehensible.[36]

Thus, theological reflection is to be understood as the precipitate of spiritual decision, spiritual decision arising out of dialogue not only with the preacher, but with God.

We will pass over a discussion of *Die Atomwaffe als Frage an die christliche Ethik*, (Nuclear Arms as a Question to Christian Ethics), 1958, not because it is not important in the sequence of Thielicke's writings, but because it may be included as another of his efforts to deal with great ethical problems. We emphasize that Thielicke felt the necessity for dealing with this great problem of modern times. This is in line with his general principle of dealing with contemporary problems and contemporary needs as they arise.

Das Leben kann noch einmal beginnen; ein Gang durch die Bergpredigt, (Life Can Begin Again; a Walk through the Sermon on the Mount), was published in its present form in 1958. The sermons had been preached originally in Stuttgart in the postwar years of 1946-1948. The series had gone through three earlier editions before the present edition was published. "References to definite events and conditions prevailing at the time when they were first delivered which would no longer be understood or which have lost their interest, have been eliminated."[37] The English edition, *Life Can Begin Again*; Sermons on the Sermon on the Mount, 1963, thanks to John W. Doberstein's excellent translation, preserves most of the author's original color and meaning. Here is a series of sermons which one can read and ponder, and then find no adequate way of summarizing them. Thielicke, in his introduction, says, "in the Sermon on the Mount we should consider less the piercing radicality of its directions and give more consideration to the Figure who is speaking here and has a definite purpose in view when he speaks in these radical terms."[38] What is this ultimate purpose? This is what Thielicke seeks to find in the Sermon on the Mount.

> The radical, straight, earnest road to which we are directed, the entrance to which is a very narrow gate, is not so laid out that it will *lead* us into a new future . . . . On the contrary, instead of fostering the illusion that we can bring about a new world situation and a new future by a radical exertion of the will, the Sermon on the Mount says to us: a future has been *given* to you, the air is full of promises, the ship of your life and history itself is sailing toward a harbor where you are expected and your safety assured.[39]

The future has already begun. Something has happened that makes it possible for you to begin again. He says it is the purpose of the book to tell about the miracle of this possibility, the possibility of beginning again. This he does in the fifteen sermons of the series on the Sermon on the Mount.

We come now to the first series of sermons prepared especially for delivery to the assembly of listeners who gathered on Saturdays and Sundays on one week-end a month to hear Thielicke preach at Michaelis. He had previously completed the series on *Das Bilderbuch Gottes,* on the parables of Jesus, on which most of the work had been done some years before his coming to Hamburg.

In 1957 he began the series on the first eleven chapters of Genesis, which he called *Wie die Welt begann; der Mensch in der Urgeschichte der Bibel,* which was published in 1960, after the entire series had been delivered in Michaelis. This series was published in America in the same year under the title *How the World Began—Man in the First Chapters of the Bible.* The book contains 18 sermons, an introductory chapter and a "Postscript for Theological Readers." It is Thielicke's attempt to come to grips with the questions and problems directed at men of faith in the setting of a great secular city and a modern university.

In a letter to Dr. Doberstein, the translator, Thielicke states his aims as follows:

(1) to hew out the message of the texts as in any proper sermon,

(2) to enter into the current discussion of the relationship between the Old and the New Testament by this means of preaching as a Christian on Old Testament texts, and

(3) to help people to grapple with the intellectual difficulties they face in this world today in which the antitheses of faith and thought, kerygma and cosmogony, religion and science create barriers for doubters and misgivings for believers.[40]

Thielicke himself says the book is concerned with only one question: What does it mean to believe? But in the next sentence he says it is also a question of *against what* I believe, meaning against what obstacles, against what misunderstandings, against what distortions. He gives this clue as to how we will deal with misunderstandings in the following sentence.

Often misunderstandings are based upon the fact that we confuse the figurative, mythical, ancient-cosmological forms of expression in these texts of the first chapters of Genesis with the thing itself, instead of seeing in them the code language of a time long past which we must translate into the clear words of our own language. In this way the biblical form of expression, which ought to be translated for some very elementary news which is of immense importance to us, becomes for many of us an iron curtain that hides them from our view and cuts them off from our ears like a soundproof wall.[41]

It is interesting that these words are taken from the written introduction to the book and not from one of the sermons. They provide the guide lines for his dealing with the misunderstandings, but he seldom if ever talks this way in the sermons. We raise the question, why is it that the educated and the uneducated, the men of very simple faith as well as the scholars all seem to feel that Thielicke is in their theological camp? The answer is to be found with the way he handles the problems of biblical interpretation.

Let us take an example from sermon number nine in this series.[42] Numerous examples of the same general approach could be cited. This sermon is entitled "How Evil Came into the World." To explain Thielicke's method we must give a little of the continuity of the sermon. Thielicke begins by reading the biblical account from Genesis 3:1-7,—the subject has already been announced. The text, of course, includes the conversation of Eve with the serpent. On finishing the text Thielicke recalls a vivid wartime story in which twenty boys from a Latin school were manning an anti-aircraft battery. Thielicke had repeatedly gone out to teach these boys at their gun position and had come close to them. Death struck the father of one of the boys in a low-level strafing attack on the emplacement. The father had been visiting the young men and was killed just before Thielicke arrived one evening. Although he tried to comfort the boys, he felt utterly helpless. Later he walked home through the beautiful countryside, which he describes in the most vivid terms. How delusive, this scene compared with the scene of death he had just witnessed.

He then returns to his text, to Adam and Eve, the scene in the garden, its contrasts so like the contrasts surrounding his listeners. And then he says,

> At first, as an intellectual living in the atomic age, one is inclined to take offense at many of the mythical features of this story—for example, the idea of a serpent that can speak. But scarcely has this skepticism begun to stir when we are so compelled to listen to *what* the serpent says that the feeble protest of our intellect is simply thrust aside.[43]

He then asks the question: "Do not all of us know certain scenes in our lives that recur in this story of a temptation?" Thielicke asks many more pointed questions and speaks about how the devil or the old serpent carries on his deceiving work but from Thielicke there is no more mention of the problem of the talking serpent until near the end of the sermon. There is so much of reality in the remainder of the sermon, and the devil becomes so contemporary that it is doubtful that anyone listening to Thielicke would give thought to the serpent talking or to the *mythical* aspect of the Bible story. It is not that the serpent stops talking, but that most of what he says is so up to date that we forget our original objection to the story. On the concluding page of the sermon Thielicke asks,

> Has any one of us been bothered during this chapter by the fact that he is unable to

imagine a serpent that can speak and think? No, the reason why we can find no peace, the reason why we cannot find God lies at this *one* point in our life, this *one* tree in the midst of the garden, which we refuse to allow to be forbidden. What is this point in your life and my life?[44]

In this way Thielicke helps his listeners to deal with their objections, their misunderstandings of the biblical account, and at the same time fulfills his other purposes in preaching.

One collection of short sermons and meditations not published in a book form in Germany was edited and translated by Doberstein and published in America in 1962. The title of the book is *Christ and the Meaning of Life*. Most of these messages were presented over radio and television. They have been arranged in the general order of the church year. They show Thielicke to be as much the master of the short form of address as he undoubtedly is of the longer forms of address. Whether Thielicke's style of delivery is as effective on radio and television as it is in the pulpit or behind the lectern is another question. But this does not come in question in this excellent book of short sermons and meditations.

Lectures on Freedom and Related Subjects

Thielicke has made scores of addresses to groups, conventions, worker's unions, professional organizations and clubs, as well as to religious and educational associations. One of the subjects with which he has been most concerned is the matter of "freedom." His address delivered on the occasion of his assuming the rectorate of the University of Hamburg, November 9, 1960, was entitled *Was heisst Freiheit?* (What Is Freedom?) It was printed in booklet form by the university in 1961.

In 1962 Thielicke and Doberstein collaborated on the publication of an edition of an English collection of ten of Thielicke's addresses, lectures, articles, and study papers on the general subject of freedom, entitled *The Freedom of the Christian Man.* The first address in this book is the English translation of *Was heisst Freiheit?* under the title, "What is Freedom?" To indicate the range of Thielicke's interest in "freedom" we list herewith the titles of the addresses included in this collection. They are as follows: (1) What is Freedom? (2) Ideals in a Free Society, (3) The Threat of Modern Society to Freedom, (4) The Antithesis of Free Society, (5) What Will We Say to the Young Communists on X-Day? (6) Freedom and Love of One's Neighbor: A Critique of the Idea of "Human Relations," (7) Freedom of Decision: The Impossibility of Casuistry in Ethical Christianity, (8) Man's Freedom and God's Rule: On the Meaning of History, (9) The Freedom of Preaching in the Age of the Masses, (10) The Freedom of Man and the Autonomy of Historical Process.

Another now famous address in the same general subject area is *Thielicke's Deutschland Demokratie oder Vaterland; Die Rede an die Deutschen,* delivered on June 6, 1962, before the *Bundestag* in Bonn and in a nationwide radio and television broadcast. Thousands of recordings of this address have been sold. The Address is published in a 110 page booklet by the above title, which includes an analysis of the letter writing response to the address.

Von der Freiheit ein Mensch zu sein, (The Freedom to be Human), an address delivered at the anniversary of the death of Professor and Mrs. Scholl, which was held at the University of Munich on the 22nd of February, 1963, is another example of Thielicke's devotion to freedom.

Another little book of 126 pages in the same category as the above is the book entitled *Der Einzelne und der Apparat* (The Individual and the Machine), 1964. A secondary title of the book translated into English is *Man's Freedom in a Technical Age.* The chapter headings indicate its content and the fact that it belongs in the general group we are discussing: (1) The Individual and the Machine, (2) What is Freedom? (3) Is Technocracy Devilish? (4) An Illustration: Freedom and Leisure, and (5) The Final Aspect: History and Judgment.

One can read all of these lectures, centering as they do on subjects in the general area of *freedom,* without feeling that Thielicke is unduly repeating himself. How can this be? This is due in part to the thoroughness with which Thielicke prepares each separate lecture, undoubtedly having in mind a specific audience and special emphases to fit the situation.

Thielicke's ability to do the necessary research on an address such as the one on Marxism, entitled "The Antithesis of Free Society,"[45] is most exemplary. He quotes communist authorities from Marx-Engels to Mao Tse-tung, including more than a score of other writers and their works to develop an authentic picture of the communist ideology.

In no other one of his books does he range so widely for his authorities and arguments as in *The Freedom of the Christian Man.* An interesting point is that almost invariably he draws on his extensive knowledge of the writings of Luther to bring his argument to a head. Luther's concept of brotherly love is a necessary ingredient of a Christian view of freedom. Thielicke concludes that "freedom is possible only within certain limitations and a framework of obligations, if it is not to become a playground of neutral values and thus a force that produces mere chaos."[46]

In several of these lectures he quotes Paul de Lagarde, when he says, "Freedom does not consist in our being able to do what we want to do, but in becoming what we should become."[47]

Thielicke is clearly skeptical about the chances for continued freedom in a *secularized* so-called free and democratic West, as for example in the following paragraph from "What Will We Say to the Young Communists?"

> It would appear to me that these terms *free* and *democratic* come close to being mere cliches. Rather I start from the fact that the so-called Western world acquired its intellectual and moral substance in encounter with the figure of Jesus Christ and that therefore the secularized West is like a machine whose motor has been turned off but still goes on turning for a time, though really only for a limited time. It may be that the de-Christianized West is looking for some other sources of motive power in order to gain new impulse.[48]

At this point he discusses the substitute religion of existentialism and other substitutes with which to face the young communists and how the West really has nothing with which to counter communism apart from the message of the freedom of the children of God.[49]

Even in Thielicke's lecture on "The Threat of Modern Society to Freedom" before the Overseas Club of Hamburg there is a solid religious base. The message ends with the use of Thielicke's favorite illustration, The Prodigal Son, which in this case he uses to illustrate the loss of freedom and its regaining.[50]

The Travel Books

At this point an exception is being made in that we are going to discuss in a group the books Dr. Thielicke has written about his travel experiences. Actually we have already departed slightly from the chronological order we have generally followed in this chapter in discussing Thielicke's writings, in that we discussed his various available lectures on the subject of *freedom* in a group, before discussing his first travel books, two of which were written and published before most of the lectures discussed in the *freedom* group.

The first of the travel books, *In Amerika ist alles anders,* (In America Everything is Different), was published in 1957 after Thielicke's 1956 visit to America.[51] His second travel book, *Vom Schiff aus gesehen,* was published in 1959, shortly after his journey to the Far East in a freighter. This book was made available to American readers in 1962 under the title *Voyage to the Far East.*

As indicated in Table 2, Page 97, these two books have proved to be quite popular with Thielicke listeners. This is partly understandable from the point of view that there is something of a fan club type of interest in the author's activities. Some listeners also keep scrap books of newspaper clippings on his views and activities reported by the press.

However, the travel books are interestingly written and are worthy of note on their own.

This is most certainly true of a later book by Thielicke, written after his half year sojourn in America in 1963, and entitled *Gespräche über Himmel und Erde, Begegnungen in Amerika.* The English translation, *Between Heaven and Earth: Conversations with American Christians,* appeared almost simultaneously with the German version. As the title indicates, this book is less a travel book and more of a book on "conversations" with American Christians. The conversations center on (1) The Bible and God, (2) Historical Criticism on the Bible, (3) Understanding the Bible, (4) The Virgin Birth, (5) Speaking in Tongues, (6) The Fate of Unbelievers, (7) Racial Integration, (8) The Nazi Regime, and (9) a discussion with journalists and students on "What Is the Most Important Question of Our Time?" The book is written from comprehensive notes taken at the time of the many conversations engaged in by the author during the six-month period of his visit in America. He uses the question and answer method to present his material. The nature of the questions selected and the answers given provide an access to the mind and heart of Dr. Thielicke not found in any of his other books.

His reactions to his shipmates in *Voyage to the Far East* provide another index to the mind and heart of the author. Repeatedly in his diary he refers to his concern for the sailors on the ship. One evening he wrote about his feelings as follows:

> I am not at all satisfied with myself this evening. Should I not have said more to the men than I did? Or am I too impatient? Is it possible to speak to them seriously at all, slightly befuddled as they are by alcohol? God alone knows what I have done wrong again . . . I went to bed tonight with some oppressive thoughts on my mind. I wanted to make this voyage in order to see something from shipboard. But now I am coming more and more to look *into* the ship and meet the people on it. I am by no means sure that Asia will present me with greater or more moving questions than does this floating microcosm.[52]

Literally scores of illustrations from the travel books could be given to show how Thielicke is impelled to deal with problems wherever he finds them, and how he tries, within the framework of his ethical-theological position to work out an approach to their solution. Furthermore, he is interested not only in problems as such, but in the people—in the individuals, in sailors, students, fundamentalists, in the persons who have problems. He is, of course, vitally interested in spelling out his position on such theological matters as verbal inspiration,[53] the Virgin Birth,[54] and historical criticism,[55] and on ethical problems such as those involved in race[56] and sex.[57]

One further point needs to be made. The travel books give added proof of Thielicke's boundless energy, which after all helps to make possible the prodigious amount of work that he has accomplished. All this leads to the conclusion that the *travel books* are a valuable source of information on the mind and heart of Thielicke, and a valuable aid to us in our attempt to understand his power as a preacher.

Thielicke's Recent Writings

Under the classification of recent writings, using these terms somewhat loosely, there are five books left to be discussed. These five books are *Auf Kanzel und Katheder,* two books on preaching, and two series of sermons.

The first of the five is already quite familiar to anyone who has followed the development of the study to this point, for we have used freely the material from *Auf Kanzel und Katheder,* especially in Chapter 3, in the presentation of "Helmut Thielicke, the Man."[58] In addition to the biographical material in the first section, the book contains the report on Thielicke's first American visit,[59] a number of Thielicke's annual form letters to his friends, two articles entitled "Memories of Two Teachers," and a "Conclusion" to the entire collection.

As in the case of his annual letters, Thielicke

considers the publication of this book in 1965 as a report to his friends, and an expression of his appreciation for the privilege of relating in his life the two vocational elements, the pulpit and the lectern. The remaining four books we shall look into here, as much as any of the books Thielicke has written, give evidence of his effectiveness in relating pulpit and lectern.

We turn now to the two books dealing primarily with preaching. The first is *Vom geistlichen Reden; Begegnung mit Spurgeon,* published in Germany in 1961, and in America in 1963. The English title is *Encounter with Spurgeon.* The second book, primarily on preaching, entitled *Leiden an der Kirche* (The Trouble with the Church), was published in German and in English in 1965. We reserve the discussion of these two books until the first section of the next chapter of this study, entitled "The Preacher—Principles and Practices," for the first part of which these books provide our best printed resources.

This leaves only the two series of sermons. The series of 20 sermons entitled *Ich Glaube* (I Believe) was begun in 1961, and published in 1965. This series, preached at Michaelis, reflects the fact that Thielicke has for several years been simultaneously working on a larger work he calls his *Dogmatik* (dogmatics).

Ich Glaube is composed of sermons based on

a phrase by phrase use of the Apostles' Creed
for texts and for continuity in the sequence of
sermons. As in the case of the previous series
of sermons preached at Michaelis, this series
also commanded the attention of a packed
sanctuary. There was a difference however. It
was no longer necessary to preach the same
sermon twice to provide room for most of the
would-be listeners. This fact alone should not
cause us to conclude that there was less interest in the actual content of the sermons on the
part of those accommodated by the available
space in the great church. But there is reason
to believe that these sermons represent something of a change in emphasis, and that their
appeal is on a somewhat less popular level.

In reading this series one is aware that the
material and the style of the sermons is more
in the vein of reasoned argument than are
most of the sermons of former series. Nevertheless, this is preaching, this is witnessing,
and it is done in the context of a worship service. Thielicke is careful to explain that the
sermons are not put into the exact argumen-
tative style one would expect in a dogmatic
treatise.[60] Because Thielicke believes that his
congregation is made up of harbor workers,
buyers, merchants, students, pietists, new-
heathen, converted people, and skeptics, his
messages are written to have a wide appeal
to all classes of people. It is quite true that this
series has fewer *strange words (Fremdwörter)*

than his most recent series entitled *Wie modern darf die Theologie sein?* which we have yet to discuss. This may only be due to the nature of the subjects of the two series, rather than because of a planned strategy concerning the use of language, or a drift toward the language of the intellectual class.

Returning to the content of *Ich Glaube*—the theme of the prodigal son is found here also, but more emphasis is given to the older brother who *could not love*.[61] Reconciliation and love become dominant themes in this series.[62]

Thielicke does not avoid the difficult parts of the Creed such as "He descended into hell." He discusses the related question, "Where Are the Dead?" His conception of hell may not satisfy every conservative scholar, but it should be helpful to modern men who seek answers to one of the perennial biblical questions.[63]

In his discussion of the resurrection as in other sermons on the Creed, he returns repeatedly to the "glory" and the "splendor" of Jesus. He says that we should not dispute with doubting Thomases, but should show them something of the glory of Christ, as we understand him, perhaps even without words, with the simple language of deeds.[64]

Throughout the series on the Creed Thielicke is *preaching* in the best sense of the word, *not lecturing*. Every sermon is a confrontation of men with God, with Christ, or with the Holy Spirit. The last sermon ends with one of the

most stern appeals in all of Thielicke's printed
sermons. The appeal is based on the parable
of the rich man, to whom it was said, "Tonight
thy soul will be required of thee." Thielicke
ends his appeal with "Where do you stand?
Tonight, tonight."

As already indicated, *Wie modern darf die
Theologie sein?* (How Modern Dare Our Theology Be?) is the title of the series of sermons
preached by Thielicke at Michaelis during
1966 and 1967. As explained in Chapter 2, on
Page 36 of this study, this is the only series of
Thielicke sermons heard in person by the
writer. He saw and heard and felt the response
of great congregations both in Michaelis and
in the vast *Sportpalast* in Hannover, where
Thielicke spoke at the 1967 *Kirchentag*. In this
series Thielicke was walking where angels
fear to tread. He was doing what many people
had challenged him to do, that is, dealing with
the problems raised by modern theology.

The series of four sermons has been published with an introduction, "to the reader,"
and with a conclusion addressed to theological
readers, in a 106 page booklet with a subtitle
which may seem a little pretentious. It reads
Four Models of Present Day Proclamation.
Whether the subtitle was the author's idea or
the publisher's idea to call attention to the
series, is probably not important. One may
honestly conclude that Thielicke purposely,

conscientiously prepared these sermons as models which he hoped would be helpful to both laymen and preachers.

Thielicke assumes that only "small belief" and fear of loss of faith cause some persons to avoid raising the problems of modern theology. He also assumes that when the problems which motivate us out of historical-critical textual research, in *Formgeschichte,* in the problem area of faith and history (*Geschichte*), as well as in the area of hermeneutical methodology— when these problems are of a theological nature, that they must at any rate be preached and it must be possible for them to be a part of the proclamation.[65]

To show how this can be done is what Thielicke sets himself to do in these sermons. His messages are directed to all who have heard about the conflict over the meaning of modern theology, to the searcher and the questioner as well as to those rooted in the faith.

How does Thielicke deal with the problem he sets himself? To explain satisfactorily how he attempts to carry out his purpose is practically impossible without at length actually doing what he does in the course of the four one-hour sermons. The following paragraphs are the result of an attempt to give some indication of his method.

First, he chooses each of his four subjects so that each deals with a central question relative to the conflict over the meaning of modern theology for proclamation. His subjects are:

   (1) How Modern Dare Our Theology Be?
   (2) How Dependable are the Biblical Reports of Jesus Acts?
   (3) Wonder Over the Report of a Miracle.
   (4) What Is to be Held Concerning the Biblical Words About the Future?

Next, he chooses the most effective texts to be tied to the subject both for the purpose of presenting his message and for illustrating his method. The first thing he does with the texts is to put them into Germanized language. He calls it a *Verdeutschung* of the text. Thielicke says he is himself surprised how modern this makes the text sound, even though he was not striving for modernity.[66] The result is a kind of German J. B. Phillips effect.

Following the reading of the text, Thielicke opens up the question to be investigated. He shows how the very fact of the *practice of preaching* illustrates the need in each generation for interpretation and reinterpretation of the words of Scripture. He provides a background for the discussion of the questions raised by modern theology. It should be emphasized that he does not shy away from raising the difficult questions presented by modern theology. He raises them in the context of a warm evangelical faith in the power of the Christian gospel,—the Christian gospel as seen in the witness of the New Testament writers and in the lives of Christians in all ages.

He is appreciative of the efforts of modern biblical scholars to give relevance to the record by reinterpreting its meaning. He even speaks with respect of a particularly incisive and descriptive writing by Jacobsen, who is an atheist.[67] At one point in the first sermon he warns against those pious people who see nothing but a "sink of corruption in all that is related to modern theology and who see its representatives as masks of Satan. Such people may find themselves in trouble in the day of judgment because of the idle words and the often false witness which they have launched against their neighbors."[68]

He aims to get listeners to think in terms of essential beliefs. What is essential for faith?

Christ is not to be found in the adherence to a literalistic faith in the texts of scripture, but at the cross—in the vision of one who suffered the death on the cross for us, and broke through the front (wall) of death on the third day. He is not our savior because he performed this or that miracle.

Thielicke shows how Matthew works into the story of the stilling of the waves his witness as to whom he believes Jesus to be. Matthew believes that Christ is in the boat with all who believe; therefore, ultimately no evil can happen to the disciples or to believers. Thielicke concludes that Matthew did not falsify the story

of Jesus; he simply put into the story the totality of his knowledge of Jesus.[69]

Thielicke aims to make his explanations
"faith-producing." For example, he writes:

> We do not believe in the miracles which
> prove Christ to be our Lord, but we believe
> on the lord who does miracles, who is able
> to change our lives, who lets us see every-
> thing in a new way and who today is on the
> spot with his wonders, with his protection,
> and with his inexplicable leadership.[70]

On the reliability of the written records concerning Jesus, Thielicke writes:

> When the one who brings the message is
> always in it as one who has been gripped
> by it, when he is not a neutral onlooker in a
> box seat, but so to speak is also on the stage,
> when he is involved in the drama and can
> not do otherwise than to tell his own story
> with the story of Jesus, then one can scarce-
> ly brush aside his report as fiction or as the
> product of phantasy.[71]

Furthermore, no one can confess Christ in
such a way that he does not at the same time
acknowledge what Christ is to him, and therefore speaks of himself. This is the profound
and essential reason why "the evangelists
could not just report in the simple historical
sense, but they had to make a witness; they
proclaim and preach, they speak as those who
are *engaged*."[72] The German word for engaged
has the sense of "taken in by." Who Jesus Christ

is, concludes Thielicke, I can experience only as a disciple.

This chapter must be concluded with the reflection that just as Thielicke's work on the *Ethik* had its effect on his preaching during the years of his labors upon it, so his present effort in writing a larger *Dogmatik* is effecting his preaching as already seen in the two volumes of *Ich Glaube*, and *Wie modern darf die Theologie sein?* For Thielicke deals in his preaching with the problems which are commanding his attention most at the time. For the present he sees a great need in the area of conflict surrounding modern theology.

NOTES AND REFERENCES

[1]Note: English titles are underlined only when the title represents a book published in English.

[2]This is necessary because some of the German books are translated only in part, or one book may become a part of several English books.

[3]See K & K, p. 11. [Reference here is to his one year study of the problem of tragedy, which, he says, is still a part of a lecture cycle in his classes.]

[4]*Ibid.*, p. 16.

[5]K & K, p. 31.

[6]*Ibid.*, p. 26.

[7]*Ibid.*

[8]This book was not available to the writer for study.

[9]K & K, p. 38.

[10]H.T., *Man in God's World*, p. 184.

[11]See question number 52 in the G P C Test, on page 251.

[12]H. T., *A little Exercise for Young Theologians*, p. 28.

[13]H. T., *Nihilism* . . . , p. 105.

[14]*Ibid.*, p. 115.

[15]*Ibid.*, p. 142.

[16]*Ibid.*, p. 145.

[17]*Ibid.*, p. 142.

[18]K & K, p. 185. [Volume I of the *Theological Ethics* was finally published in the U.S.A. in 1966.]

[19]See Table 2, p. 97.

[20]Titles in parentheses are not published in English.

[21]This is not the same book as the one above published in English under the same title.

[22]In this book, published in 1965, Thielicke discusses a malady of modern preaching which he calls *Docetism*. We return to this subject in Chapter 5, page 160.

[23]*Ibid.*, p. 78.

[24]H. T., *Die Evangelische Kirche und die Politik*, 1953, p. 12.

[25]*Ibid.*, p. 28.

[26]*Ibid.*, pp. 57-62.

[27]See Table 2, p. 97.

[28]P. 40.

[29]P. 99.

[30]P. 113.

[31]See p. 171.

[32]K & K, p. 26.

[33]P. 26.

[34]See his Chapter IX, p. 28.

[35]P. 33.

[36]P. 34.

[37]See Thielicke's introduction, "To the Reader," p. xv.

[38]*Ibid.,* p. xiii.

[39]*Ibid.,* p. xiv.

[40]See "Translator's Introduction," pp. vii-viii.

[41]P. 11.

[42]The sermon begins on p. 121.

[43]P. 123.

[44]P.135.

[45]H. T., *The Freedom of the Christian Man,* pp. 83-108.

[46]*Ibid.,* p. 27.

[47]*Ibid.,* p. 10. See also H. T., *Deutschland Demokratie oder Vaterland,* p. 17, and p. 27.

[48]H. T., *The Freedom of the Christian Man,* p. 118.

[49]*Ibid.,* p. 124.

[50]*Ibid.,* p. 81.

[51]In 1965 it was republished as a separate chapter in *Kanzel und Katheder,* pp. 81-126.

[52] H. T., *Voyage to the Far East,* p. 17.

[53]H. T. *Between Heaven and Earth,* p. 6-7.

[54]*Ibid.,* p. 74-78.

[55]*Ibid.,* p. 23-29.

[56]*Ibid.,* Chapter VII, especially p. 122-134.

[57]*Ibid.,* p.187.

[58]See footnote, p. 51.

[59]This is the report first published as *In Amerika ist alles anders.* See p. 81 in K & K.

[60]See his introduction, p. 14.

[61]*Ibid.,* p. 138.

[62]*Ibid.,* p. 154.

[63]*Ibid.,* p. 175.

[64]*Ibid.,* p. 239.

[65]See p. 101.
[66]P. 8.
[67]P. 37.
[68]P. 15.
[69]P. 67.
[70]P. 68.
[71]P. 48.
[72]P. 49.

Chapter 5

THE PREACHER—PRINCIPLES AND PRACTICE

The purposes of this chapter are (1) to discuss Thielicke's views, ideals, and principles on preaching, and (2) to relate these to the *Twenty Lay Expectation Factors.* In the next chapter we will seek to illustrate through a representative Thielicke sermon how his preaching meets the expectation of the listeners. For the first part of this chapter we will lean heavily on two books written by Dr. Thielicke: *The Trouble with the Church,*[1] and *Encounter with Spurgeon,*[2] his two books most concerned with discussion of preaching.

When Thielicke wrote *The Trouble with the Church,* he had preaching in mind almost constantly, but not exclusively. The book is, as the title states, an analysis of what is wrong with the church; however, most of what is wrong involves preaching. If in this chapter we tend to ignore parts of the diagnostic and analytical emphases of the book, it is because our purpose here is to highlight the positive suggestions made by Thielicke in regard to the renewal of the church through preaching and because we are concerned with relating his ideals and

principles in preaching to the main concern
of the study, namely, the *Lay Expectation Factors*.

Thielicke's Ideals and Principles in Preaching and How They Relate to Lay Expectation Factors

Credibility—

One of the chief concerns of Thielicke is also
one of the chief concerns of the laymen. When
Thielicke discusses "The Plight of Preaching,"[3]
his first concern is "Our Credibility."[4] In an
age of high-powered advertising and public
relations departments, in an age when men and
women have forgotten neither the deception
exercised on them by the forces of Nazi tyranny
nor the impotency of the average minister in
dealing with the insidious spread of the Nazi
revolution, and in an age when survival depends
on a constant sifting of voices, and as Thielicke
says, on a "very sensitive instinct for routine
phrases,"[5]—in such an age *credibility* has become a matter of utmost importance.

In the weakened religious consciousness of
modern men there is a general tendency to rele-
gate the church and the minister to the peri-
phery of life.

> But it is not only the *place* where the preach-
> ing is done that has been so dubiously rel-
> egated to the periphery of life and thus in
> an organic sense displaced. Actually preach-

ing itself has decayed and disintegrated to
the point where it is close to the stage of
dying.[6]

If all this is true, then it is not only logical, but
it is imperative that credibility should become
a matter of grave concern to one who is deeply
involved in the training of ministers, as is Dr.
Thielicke.

What is credibility and how is it achieved?
From the point of view of the layman, credibility is as easily defined as any lay expectation factor. The layman simply asks: "Can
I believe what he says? Can I trust him? Is
what he says believable?" However, when we
attempt to answer the question as to how what
a minister says becomes credible, we find no
simple answer. The answer lies in a number
of areas. An obvious one is in the matter of the
adequacy of the preacher's information. When
the correctness of his use of sources is questioned, his problem may lie in the area of
preparation, in a lack of ability to use his
sources, or in a lack of application of effort to
his task. It is possible that the preacher's
credibility may be lowered by careless preparation without the listener being aware of
his lack of preparation.

When lack of credibility lies in the area of
veracity and in the adequacy of his sources, it
is closely related to another L E F, namely the
basis and use of authority. Even when he

claims God or the Bible as his source and authority for what he says his credibility may be questioned, depending on how he uses the Bible to back up his claims in his proclamation of his message.

Then there is the whole area of the non-verbal in communication. A secular writer has written that anyone who is critical of a speaker "keeps constantly and uppermost the connections between two levels: the verbal and the non-verbal, the worlds of the speakable and the unspeakable."[7] Anyone who is critical seeks to check the language at every point for the relationship it has to the discoverable facts of life.

When credibility or lack of credibility is related to the area of the non-verbal it is closely related to several other L E Fs, namely, *delivery* and *personality* factors. Roger Brown has written a significant book on the covariation of linguistic behavior with other kinds of events. One of his most significant emphases centers on the importance of what he calls the *expressive function of language.*

> All aspects of linguistic behavior are *expressive.* Indeed, all kinds of behavior are expressive. . . . The same utterance is simultaneously expressive and referential. . . . We have learned to attend to both reference and expression.[8]

How is this related to credibility? Brown goes on to explain that because of the fact that listeners have learned to penetrate beyond the words of a speaker for meaning, by having learned the referents for certain expressive symptoms, they can penetrate to a truth about a person which he has not intended to reveal. This has profound meaning for preaching. If credibility is made up of the expressive elements of speech, and if it is made up of nonverbal elements as well as of the overt expression of ideas and images, then Thielicke's warning against a "Dichotomy of Christian Existence" must be taken seriously.[9] Thielicke writes:

> So if our preaching has lost life and vitality compared with that of earlier generations, if indeed it is almost dead, it is not because we are less skillful rhetorically or mentally duller and stuffier then our fathers, but rather because of this dichotomy in our existence. The fault lies in a pathological condition in our spiritual life.[10]

Thus, for Thielicke the question of credibility does not hinge on whether the preacher might be accused of gross hypocrisy; it is a question of what it means to be convinced of something and to advocate it as truth. In this connection he says:

> It is not sufficient for us that the preacher is subjectively imbued with the correctness of his convictions and that he therefore is not a conscious hypocrite. . . . In order to

> be able to form a judgment concerning his
> credibility . . . we would have to know
> whether he lives, whether he really "exists,"
> in the house of the dogmas he proclaims.[11]

Credibility may be closely related to the quality of tone a man uses in his preaching. Thielicke asks why it is that a certain minister can talk about Kafka or Tennessee Williams and be "all there," but when he enters the pulpit he loses that natural and casual tone which normally indicates that what is being said has become a natural and obvious part of his intellectual organism.

> But when he talks about "sacred" things,
> the very timbre of his voice (though it has
> not a trace of "pulpit tone") shows that he is
> talking about something which has been
> brought in from some faraway region,
> something that now lies like a foreign body,
> like a meteor from another planet in the
> normal landscape of his life.[12]

The question is: Does what a minister says and the way he says it reveal that he lives in the house of his own preaching, or has he settled down somewhere beside it, so that the center of gravity in his life lies elsewhere? The genuine personal tone will be immediately discernible when the speaker himself is in what he says, if he gives of himself and puts his whole heart into it.

What about the preacher's awareness of this? Thielicke writes:

Naturally, the preacher himself knows
this, even if he is one of these unfortunates
who live "alongside" of their message. Then
sometimes—and again not hypocritically
but in the honest belief that it is as it should
be—the vox humana is blended with the
trick rhetorical note and he steps on the
swell to produce the ring of conviction. For
he knows theologically that the gospel demands the whole man. So the full phonetic
effect must be produced and the genuine
note of the heart must be sounded.[13]

To understand the longing for credibility,
Thielicke believes that one must also look at
the inner situation of the potential hearer. As
he sees the situation, people today are not
generally asking the question: "Where shall I
learn to believe?" To ask that question, a person would already have to know by and large
what faith is and what it could mean for his
own life. Rather people are asking, "Where
can I find credible witnesses?"

Because the layman's question has changed,
the church's emphasis must change. It is
strange to hear Thielicke, a Lutheran, say, "I
believe that hitherto, Protestantism has given
far too much thought to faith and far too little
to the problem of credibility."[14] He then repeats that credibility has to do with the relation
of the faith to the person and thus with the question whether a person is really practicing his
faith. It would seem that the emphasis should

rather be placed on a "credible faith," which is
what Thielicke seems to say when he adds, "No,
it is rather a question whether he really practices his faith."[15]

Thielicke points out that this theme, the relation of faith to credibility, is not a new one. It
is a theme of the New Testament, which speaks
repeatedly of the vicious dichotomy of the devout man and the preacher. "Once one sees this
problem one finds it everywhere, from the Gospels to the Epistle of James. We need only to
think of the story of the Good Samaritan."[16] He
points out how certain clerics could not relate
the wounded man to God because only their
professional schedules had anything to do with
God.

Putting this argument in still another way,
the question of the credibility of the witness
cannot be ignored because "All the really vital
questions that touch the depths of existence
enter man's consciousness through the medium of persons in whom these questions are,
as it were, incarnated."[17]

How does this relate to preaching? In Thielicke's discussion of the *how* of preaching as
taught by Spurgeon, he writes: "When we talk
about the *how* of preaching in Spurgeon, it
would be quite wrong simply to call attention
to his brilliant application of exemplary rules
and techniques and then appeal to preachers
to imitate him."[18] He goes on to explain:

. . . the real secret of the how of preaching

lies far deeper. For him who does not share this secret—that is, who does not exist at the place where this secret is to be found—the application of these rules remains out of reach, for even the how of this kind of speech is in itself nothing less than a demonstration of redemption. Tell me, not only what, but how you speak, and I will tell you whether you are sharing in redemption.[19]

Certainly Spurgeon is also talking about credibility. If we put together his idea that the *how* of preaching is only a kind of by-product of spiritual existence and Thielicke's inquisitive concern for how and what the witness lives by and how his message affects his real life, we have indeed the psychological form in which the question of credibility manifests itself concretely.

The answer to this combination question in the life and work of a preacher would tell much about how his credibility would be felt by his laymen. This brings us back to the *how* of preaching, for both Thielicke and Spurgeon believe that it is not only the *what* of the sermon that is important, but also the *how*. The question is, in what way does the *how* manifest the credibility of the message?

At least one sense in which the *how* is important is related to one of the deepest longings of our time. And that is the longing of the men of our generation for the *conversational tone,* or for the conversational tone expanded to fit the place or area of proclamation. Thielicke

emphasizes that "this age of alienated personality has an unbounded yearning for credibility
and a man's own tone."[20] He himself has continued the successful demonstration of this
ideal. We are, of course, aware that here again
we are not only speaking about credibility, but
also about those closely related factors—*manner of delivery* and *preacher's personality*—
more precisely, his pulpit personality.

Again, in a paragraph related to these three
areas Thielicke continues,

> So in a time when we are all accustomed to
> the functionary's ventriloquism there is
> simply no sense in using a particular kind
> of pulpit tone or a strained solemnity in
> order to indicate even by one's tone of voice
> that one is moving in sacred heights and in
> the precincts of ultimate earnestness, and
> that one is therefore elevated above the mis-
> ty flats of the secular slaves of opinion.[21]

He adds that in a country where the people
who listen to the mass media have been for a
long time now a part of soccer "congregations"
and have listened to margarine "liturgies," it
is impossible to rely on any kind of histrionics
for the sake of effect.

> In the deceitful atmosphere of our time
> we can speak of the unconditioned only by
> explaining quite soberly, dispassionately,
> and realistically the matter we are concerned
> with, speaking a very natural language in

an almost conversational tone. By the very fact that we do not speak in any way out of the ordinary we make it clear that the *content* of what we say is different, that God is the "wholly Other."[22]

Since credibility is of central importance to preaching and is, incidently, central to this study as an area of investigation we have written at some length about it here. We close the discussion of credibility, for the time being, with Thielicke's concluding sentence on this subject. It refers to the heart of the problem.

As long as we have not conquered the "sickness unto death," which is seated in our unconvincing Christian existence and nowhere else, all the secondary remedies are meaningless and restricted to very innocuous symptom-therapy.[23]

Practical Help for Living—

Next in our list of *Lay Expectation Factors* we turn our attention to *practical help for living* because it was rated by laymen in the Ideal Q-sort Test as next to importance to credibility.

On the part of the preacher lay expectation in this regard requires first that he must know the needs of his people. Secondly, in order to minister effectively to their needs, it requires that he be willing to do the hard work necessary in the preparation of the sermon.

The preacher knows the needs of his listeners in part through his study of the meaning of the

Christian faith and also by knowing his people
in their need. He knows their need for faith,
their need for repentance, for assurance of forgiveness, for comfort, for the knowledge of the
presence and the power of God in their lives,
and their need for understanding the purposes
of God in their lives. He may know all this only
in an academic way. Thielicke is aware of all
this.

Under the topic, "The Intellectual Demand of
Preaching," Thielicke first discusses the use
of a text and its development. In this connection
he stresses that every new text and every new
sermon compels the preacher to face afresh
the task of making it relevant and timely.[24] How
can this be done? He continued as follows:

> I must deliver the message of this text to
> people living today. And therefore I must
> know these people; I must know at what
> points they raise questions, so that I can
> "latch on" to these questions, and I must
> know where they do *not* have questions, so
> that I must first stir them up to ask the per-
> tinent questions. I must know whether they
> feel safe and secure, in order that I may shake
> them, or whether they are troubled with anx-
> iety, that I may be able to comfort and en-
> courage them.[25]

In this paragraph he speaks of specific needs
of "people living today." The preacher must
stir the people to ask the pertinent questions
as well as to know what questions they are not

asking. He must know where to "shake" them as well as to help them feel safe and secure. He must know how to comfort and encourage real people.

Thielicke follows this summary-type statement by noting the needs of several specific groups: the old ladies from the old folks home; and a contrasting group, the young people, who have their life before them. He makes suggestions on how to reach these divergent groups.

It is at this point in his discussion that Thielicke stresses "dialogue." He writes:

> Thus as a preacher I am involved in an unending dialogue with those to whom I must deliver my message. Every conversation I engage in becomes at bottom a meditation, a preparation, a gathering of material for my preaching. I can no longer listen disinterestedly even to a play in a theater without relating it to my pulpit. . . . Thus life in all its daily involvements becomes for me a thesaurus in which I keep rummaging, because it is full of relevant material for my message.[26]

If through "dialogue" he is able to understand and to seek to meet the needs of widely divergent groups in his congregation, this does not obviate the necessity to find a common denominator by which he can address the congregation as a whole. Therefore, he also asks:

> Is there not a level in man which is the same in all, that level where he is desperate

and lonely, despairing of the meaning of
existence, but also where he loves his children, cherishes his fondest wishes, and hopes
for the fulfillment of his dreams? Is there
not a dimension where all men are identical
and homogeneous? How could I ever find
it except through love which makes it possible to understand?[27]

Thus, love, in terms of I Corinthians 13 becomes the key to meeting the needs of people.

Another topic closely related to *practical help
for living* is what Thielicke speaks of as a *Docetic* view of man. We shall, however, reserve the
discussion of this problem until we take up
theological content.

Use of the Bible—

In his discussion of the "Intellectual demands
of Preaching,"[28] Thielicke begins with a description of the complex mass of operations
which need to be mastered and forced into a
unity—namely, into a sermon.

The first subject he takes up is the use of a
text. He begins, "I have before me an ancient
text, which needs to be made to speak to this
present day. . . . I must know what the text
meant in its day and what Isaiah, for example,
really intended to say in the moment he uttered
it."[29] Thielicke assumes that this will involve
a great deal of historical and philological work
"if the thing is going to be real."[30]

Historico-critical study of the Bible . . .
provides material for honest appropriation

and contemporization. But this material requires to be worked through. And in every new text and therefore in every new sermon it compels the preacher afresh to face the task of making it relevant and timely.[31]

But after spelling out the necessity for this kind of study, he warns that what happens in the pulpit must not turn out to be a lecture on Bible problems and certainly it must not remain that. On the contrary, the preacher must deliver the message of the text to people living today. It is at this point that he enters into the discussion on the necessity of knowing the people to whom he is preaching, which we have discussed in the preceding section on *practical help for living.*

He writes that preachers should engage in consultation with those who will be the hearers of the sermon, and that this means with "laymen." In this connection he speaks of his own personal experience.

> Time and again it has been my personal experience that hardly ever do we arrive at such vital, searching, and yet thematically broad discussions as when we talk over with others a text which is to be the basis of a sermon.[32]

Thus Thielicke believes in keeping up a "dialogue" between pulpit and pew.

In regard to the need for disciplined study of the text and for adequate preparation of the sermon, Thielicke had some sharp words to

say regarding one who allowed himself to
handle the Word of God sloppily, when he said,
"How shocking is the display of slovenliness
in this of all places!"[33]—referring here to the
pulpit of a large church.

Thielicke's name for the kind of preaching
he favors is *textual-thematic*. In textual-thematic preaching the preacher takes his theme
from the text itself and with its aid he formu-
lates the main point of the sermon. Thielicke
chooses this kind of preaching for three reasons:[34]

> (1) In this way one remains within the
> text and allows it to be an end in itself. One
> discovers in it a center and a periphery and
> one illuminates it on the basis of its main
> idea.
>
> (2) This way of determining the theme
> not only helps to keep the sermon true to
> the text but also helps the preacher to achieve
> order and clarity. If he merely proceeds
> word by word in the style of a homily, mak-
> ing his comments as he goes along, the
> unifying bond may easily slip away from
> him.

In summarizing this second point, he writes:

> The study of the text and theme together
> . . . makes it easier to gain clarity and or-
> der, easier to arrive at an outline which
> makes the whole sermon transparent. In
> any case, beginners can handle it more
> easily.
>
> (3) Third, this method is also more helpful

to the hearer. He retains it better and can
more readily pass it on to others.[35]

This thematic development of the sermon is
helpful most of all to hearers who are interested in a question and perhaps have no desire
to listen to any biblical exposition whatsoever.
Thielicke suggests that such listeners, who
may be among those on the fringes of the church,
may be led to recognize through textual-thematic preaching to recognize that some unexpected
problems are dealt with in the Bible.

For Thielicke it is important that the witness
is given a text to interpret and to contemporize.
That preaching is bound to its times is not a
disadvantage; it is rather a virtue. One must,
of course, assume that it does not merely ac-
commodate itself to its time and therefore become indistinguishable from it. The preacher
owes his ultimate message only to his time.
And when he has run his course, he hands the
torch on to others.[36]

An extended study of the sermons preached
by Thielicke reveals that he practices the kind
of preaching which we have described above.
This is not to say that he does not practice wide
variations of his method, but by and large his
text and theme are inseparable.

Theological Content—

In *The Trouble with the Church* Thielicke
approaches the question of the theology of the
sermon through his discussion of "dialogue"
with laymen. He looks upon theological and

spiritual exchange with laymen as a healing
spring for all the problems we face in preaching. By maintaining a living and vital point
of contact with "average men of the world"
[Thielicke's quotation marks], the preacher
avoids a great amount of sterile theorizing
about where the other person stands and what
questions must be dealt with in order to reach
him.[37]

His attitude to his preaching and to his scholarly work in this regard is clearly stated in the
following paragraph:

> Not only in his preaching but also in his
> scholarly work one can see whether a theolo-
> gian has found his question among "laymen"
> and cultivates a professional (not merely a
> general cultural or social) exchange of
> ideas with them. I believe that the reason
> why such broad areas of our theology today
> are so unfruitful and why there are so many
> barren thinkers in a time which is ripe for
> harvest is that the theologians are not doing
> much more than providing each other with
> problems and solutions.[38]

For Thielicke the "most fruitful questions
always come from outside of theology. Only
here do we have the polarity that generates
sparks."[39] What he must mean here is that the
fruitful questions arise outside of "theological
circles."

In relation to the problems raised for preaching by the professional theologians, Thielicke

believes that the gulf between the professor's lectern and the pulpit is wider and worse than the rift between the denominations and the confessions. In the latter people are beginning to speak to each other across the dividing lines, but there seems to be "hardly a bridge across the gulf between the pulpit and the professor's lectern."[40] A beginning toward solution of this problem is seen by Thielicke in the continuing conversation with the laymen. He sees this whole question as belonging in the context of a "larger problem, namely, in the whole relationship of theology to the laity, or one might say with the Reformers, in the context of the universal priesthood of believers."[41]

In a section entitled "The Decay of the Language of Preaching," among other things, Thielicke reminds us of the continuing struggle with the "reanimated relics" of the past and with pseudo-Christian concepts coming into Christianity through its Greek background. He hopes that the preacher himself is not a secret Hellenist, Idealist, or existentialist and hence that he knows the meaning of Christian terms in contrast with their original pagan meanings or their regenerated or degenerated neo-pagan significations.[42]

He is concerned about the use of the specifically Christian terms. How can they be used so as to convey what the New Testament meant by their use. Let us take, for example, the word "sin":

Where is the average person today who, when he hears the word "sin," really hears what the New Testament meant by that word? For whom today does this word still say that here man is being addressed at the point of his resistance and opposition to God, that this means man in his will to assert his autonomy, his insistence that everything centers in man, his incredible passion for security, his lostness in preoccupation with the moment and that which is tangible and immediately at hand? And yet all this must be heard when we hear the word "sin," if for no other reason than to understand that it is possible for a sinner to be at the same time an example of moral perfection and that he need by no means be a criminal, an anti-social, or even a person who lacks serious-ness.[43]

Thielicke not only explains the meaning of the term, but goes on to illustrate it. We have given this lengthy example to illustrate the point he is making and his thoroughness in the use of words with theological meaning. The point is that we need to say what we mean by even the most familiar biblical terms.

We are aware that we have been concerned here with the *delivery* of theological ideas as well as with the ideas themselves. What we are concerned with is the *words* we use to express the Word. Thielicke stresses that the more a man speaks in modern terms the more he will be heard. The more he is heard the greater will be the acceptance and the rejection of his message, the more provocative it will be, and the more emphatic will be the decisions and separations that result. "When the Word becomes flesh again, that is to say, when it enters into our own time, wearing the dress of the present, the ancient laws of the proclamation of the Word come into play and it becomes apparent that this Word is a divider of spirits and a hammer which breaks the rock in pieces."[44]

Lest we be one-sided and misrepresent Thielicke on this subject of the use of the biblical and theological terms, he also writes:

> I cannot emphasize too strongly that I have no wish to abolish the accustomed theological vocabulary and to pose as an iconoclast of the technical language of Christianity. The reference to the odor of decay that clings to the old, worn-out language applies only to the vocabulary which is simply passed on without being worked upon and digested, . . . We may also put it this way: These dogmatic words and terms are indispensable because they have stored within them the spiritual knowledge of a long history of faith. But as such receptacles they can be used only in the theological laboratory.[45]

Thus, terms which may be legitimately used in the theological laboratory become strange and inappropriate when they appear undigested and untranslated in the pulpit. In the pulpit whatever words are used must be made meaningful if the witness is to be credible.

Abstract Man: the Wrong Man to Address—

Under this heading we refer to an emphasis by Thielicke that lies in the realm of *theological content*. His emphasis is on the assertion that the preacher should speak to man as he really is, and not as "abstract man." He explains as follows:

> When a sermon does not "hit home," the reason need by no means lie in the fact that it contained no examples from life nor that it was too theoretical. On the contrary, despite all its rhetorical and pedagogical excellence, it may lie in the fact that the preacher is speaking on the basis of a Docetic anthropology and that the man of whom he is speaking and whom he is addressing does not appear in the sermon at all. Then the very hearers who are troubled by very real situational problems feel that they have been bypassed.[46]

The problem, Thielicke explains, lies in a false theology of man, which he calls *Docetism*. This Docetism, in the sphere of humanity, undoubtedly infiltrated into theology by way of existentialism. He quotes Bultmann's essay, "The Understanding of Man and the World in the New Testament and in the Greek World" to help to explain his meaning:

> The New Testament sees the monstrous power of this sphere—the "world"—it sees that the "world" with its pleasures and cares divests man of genuine care about himself,

distracting him from the search for God and the transcendent, which fixes the bounds of this world. It sees that men who are in the grip of the world trouble themselves and worry about things. . . . Man, then is indeed in the grip of the world and, so to speak, embedded in it—but for his ruin, not for his salvation.[47]

Thielicke agrees there is no doubt that all this is to be found in the New Testament, but that this is only one side of the picture. He asks a series of questions to counter this basis for a Docetic doctrine of man.

Does the New Testament not also bear witness to the freedom of man in his world? Is not the world here revealed to him as the place where God desires to meet man in His works as well as in the neighbor? Is not the world the sphere which God so loved that he 'sent his only begotten Son'? Dare one, therefore, really think of the world only as the power which holds man in its grip?[48]

Thielicke holds that "man" is man in his world and not man apart from his world. He submits that if one interprets the world only as a chain, the temptation is all to great to set forth man "in himself" *(an sich)*, and this means describing him without the chain. Then "man" is this man in his state of being unchained. "This is why the listener, the real man who is gripped and squeezed by his world and is really enchained by it, does not recognize himself in that strange, denatured, and abstract double of himself."[49]

For the minister who leans toward a Docetic anthropology, man becomes to some extent a phantom that has no meaning operationally. Thielicke will have no part of preaching to "man" as an abstraction.

How has this disaster come about? Apart from what has already been said above, Thielicke believes that "the disaster of Docetism has arisen from the fact that we leap from the text into the sermon without having traversed the field of ethics."[50] His conviction on this point was partly responsible for his writing of the *Theological Ethics.*[51]

By ethics he means not simply moral theology but an interpretation by means of Christian categories of reality, which is to say, man's being-in-the-world. His attitude to the Sermon on the Mount is consistent with this view. Thielicke states, "The Sermon on the Mount . . . places me and my whole world under its radical demands and therefore looks upon me and my world as an indivisible reality."[52]

"If it is true that we must thus see man *together* with his world and that he must by no means be isolated from it, then this has very great significance not only for theological ethics but also for the whole realm of theological anthropology."[53] Thielicke asserts that this involves a great deal of rethinking of the doctrines we preach, and he has much more to say on this subject.

But what has all this to say to preaching? Let us summarize Thielicke's discussion as follows:

(1) It demands that the preacher remain in conversation with real men and women, with individuals in and outside the church.

(2) The preacher must avoid getting mired down in discussions of esoteric problems which crop up in the conversations of theologians, and in methodological considerations unrelated to the needs of individual men and women.

(3) Illustrations used in preaching will be concerned with specific, recognizable and identifiable problems. Do not, for example, speak abstractly of self-love, but make men aware of how self-love is operative in their lives in its various manifestations as related to erotic self-love, economic self-love, or political self-love.

One of Thielicke's strengths is his ability to preach in such a way that listeners recognize themselves in the illustrations used and identify themselves with the illustrations. As a result they are able to face up to the implications of what they hear in the preaching.

Thielicke and the Liturgy—

Thielicke takes a decisive position against what he calls "the flight into liturgism." It is, he says, in the first place, a "flight from preaching."[54] But the liturgy has its place in his thinking and, of course, in the church service. The purpose of the liturgy is to give expression

to the action of the congregation. "It consti-
tutes a stationary element nourished by tradi-
tion and thus has complementary significance
for the sermon."[55] The sermon, on the other
hand, is contemporary; "it must correspond
with the time in which it is preached; it is linked
with the venture of the witness who trusts the
Spirit who moves where he wills."[56]

Rather than to participate in the flight into
"liturgism," Thielicke emphasizes that the
word has been committed to us in order that we
may pass it on. For Thielicke this means *preaching*.

The only alternative to working for an awak-
ening in preaching, for Thielicke, would be to
admit that the Reformation is finally and radi-
cally ended. This is he not ready to do.

He takes courage from the fact that the question of what the church should proclaim has by
no means ceased to be asked. On the contrary,
he writes:

> . . . our generation—especially the young
> people—is full of "hunger and thirst for
> righteousness." Wherever there is vital
> preaching (no matter whether it be Catholic
> Protestant, in summer camps or at home)
> people still come flocking to hear it, and
> again, especially the young people.[57]

For Thielicke none of the elements of preaching have more to do with whether or not preaching is vital than the theological orientation of
the preacher and the theological content of the

sermon. Moreover, *theological content* is more closely related to the *use of the Bible* in preaching than is any other factor, and the theological assumptions of the preacher are inseparably related to his *credibility,* that other most important factor.

In concluding this section on theological content, we hear Thielicke say, "Only he who dies and rises again with Christ can credibly bear witness to the death and resurrection of the Lord."[58]

We turn now to the characteristic that was ranked fifth in importance by 137 Thielicke and Lein listeners on the Ideal Q-sort, namely, *comprehensibility.*

Comprehensibility—

Aside from his stress on speaking to men in their situation and his emphasis on "dialogue," there is little in Thielicke's writings excepting by way of inference that would show his concern with comprehensibility.

In terms of "concerns" or "dimensions," he is concerned that dock workers and ship owners alike do not go away without feeling that they were included in what has been said. In this same kind of comparison he mentions other diverse groups. But he deals with the problem involved in terms of concerns, dimensions, and interests.[59]

Having listened to Thielicke lecture to students at the University of Hamburg, the writer is aware that there is a considerable difference both in vocabulary and in content of the lectures as compared to the sermons intended for the general listening audience at Michaelis. This is as one would expect it to be. But in writing about preaching Thielicke makes no big point of scaling down his vocabulary in preaching. Moreover, he does not desist from using strange words (*Fremdwörter*) altogether in his preaching. Adjustments are made in the form of additional explanations, so that his meaning becomes clear to the great majority of the listeners.

At one point Thielicke does raise the question as to how he preaches Christian truths—doctrinal truth in particular. In this connection he makes two simple points which, however, have a profound effect on preaching. The first is that every sermon must have a central point, and the second is that one cannot say everything in every sermon. His explanation follows:

> The fact is that when I express one thing *wholly* (for example, the message of the forgiveness of sins) I have thereby implicitly expressed everything else: the message of Christ's death on the cross, the resurrection, indeed, even the doctrines of creation and eschatology. All praise to the courage to be implicit! For the Christian truths are like microcosms in which the whole cosmos is portrayed. I therefore do not speak the truth in the form of quantitative expatiation upon all truths. I rather speak the truth by choosing one of its microcosms and then searching it and penetrating to its core.[60]

Upon completing the above statement Thielicke comments that "this is not only the proper way to approach the thing itself but is also suited to the hearers' capacity of *comprehension*."[61] We have underlined the word "comprehension."

By implication, there is a sense in which Thielicke's entire discussion on "Docetism" in preaching is relevant to the question of the *comprehensibility* of preaching, even as this same discussion is related to *relevance, practical help for living, use of the Bible,* and *theological content.* The point is that if one is preaching to the wrong man—abstract man— the right man will certainly not comprehend; Thielicke implies that after a few attempts he may not even be there to listen to such preaching.

Relevancy—

We have already discussed several of the areas most closely related to relevancy in preaching. Thielicke's entire discussion of Docetism in preaching is directly applicable to relevancy in preaching. If preaching is to be relevant it must be based on a Christian anthropology in which the preacher sees man *in* the world and not *apart* from the world.

Secondly, much of our discussion of *practical help for living* is pertinent to the question of relevancy. Furthermore, we have seen that relevancy is achieved through *dialogue.* And, it may as well be noted here that relevancy is one of the L E Fs that is related directly or indirectly to most of the other lay expectation factors.

Perhaps as pertinent as anything Thielicke has to say about relevancy is his discussion of "Sitz im Leben." "Sitz im Leben" literally means "relevance to life situation." For example, to ask the question: What has belief in the Trinity to do with our *Sitz im Leben,* is literally to ask: How is belief in the Trinity relevant to our life situation? In this connection Thielicke says it has been up to the church and it has been the task of theology to demonstrate the *existential relevance* of the doctrines and dogmas of the church. "The greatness of theologians like Lessing and Schleiermacher lies in the fact that they were concerned about this 'Sitz im Leben.'"[62]

Thielicke continues, "They started from the recognition that I can appropriate and receive into my existence only that which ultimately concerns me and therefore has meaning for my life."[63] It is his conviction that we are entering a new phase in the history of thought, and it seems to him that it is very important that we recognize this transition. He explains it as follows:

> Our question—in any case the question of the secularized man, in so far as he is receptive and asks the question at all—no longer begins with the given dogmas and asks what is their "Sitz im Leben." For many

the dogmas are no longer "given" at all, but are completely unreal. Our situation is rather that we are oppressed by very definite problems whose "Sitz im Leben" is quite obvious.[64]

Thielicke spells out what some of these problems are, and then says, "When we bring the gospel into contact with these given questions, the question where it has its 'Sitz im Leben' becomes anachronistic, for we are starting from this life situation!"[65] At any rate when we hear the questions, our first task is to elicit the hidden thrust of the question. In this connection Thielicke cites the example of Jesus' dialogues with people.

He always lays hold of the question with which people have approached him. But he never answers it directly, or more precisely, he never regards the question as a finished form into which the answer of his message will fit without further ado. Rather he first corrects the way the question is put, he brings out its hidden thrust, which the questioners were not yet aware of at all. Most of them did not realize what they were asking and what was oppressing them.[66]

Thus Thielicke cites the example of Jesus to illustrate how the preacher must deal with the questions in the minds of men—that is, how he must relate the gospel to the questions men ask—if he is to be relevant to the situation. To be relevant he must not only hear the questions men ask, but he must get at the basic questions.

We have already seen that Thielicke supports *textual-thematic* preaching as the best way to get at the basic questions and as the best way to bring the resources of the Bible to bear on the problems men face.

Confrontation with Decision—

Thielicke believes that the proclamation of the gospel itself presents persons with a never ending series of challenges, so that confrontation with decision occurs continually in the course of the proclamation. What may be one of his most concise statements on the subject follows:

> Whoever speaks from the pulpit as a man of our times, whoever speaks concretely (which often means very unceremoniously) and who denies himself every phonetic vestige of Docetism, he will confront men with decision, which they can not evade; through his words Jesus Christ will suddenly appear in the every-day of his hearers, and in addition to joy this will also bring a (kind of) fear before this tremendous presence.[67]

In this sense confrontation with decision often occurs without the listener being aware that he is being pressed for a decision. Moreover, by the same token, the listener may be moving toward significant decisions without consciously realizing that he is being moved toward decision. At other times under the preaching of

Thielicke the listener may be very conscious of making a decision. Although there is seldom anything like an altar-call in his preaching, there are explicit invitations, challenges, and appeals. Confrontation with decision in some form is present in every sermon.

Thielicke would say that the minister who preaches to real men, in situation, will surely confront them with the necessity for decision. However, if the preacher wittingly or unwittingly preaches to "abstract men," to the man who is not present, there can be no significant confrontation.

Thought Provoking—

Thielicke sets down no set of rules for preaching in a thought provoking manner. He does it—preaches in a thought provoking manner—so that if one would read his sermons, and could follow his example, learning to preach would be a routine matter. However, Thielicke has paid the price, and continues to pay the price, for this accomplishment. The price is best expressed in the world *preparation*—time and effort spent in preparation—combined with the response he brings to preaching in relation to the areas represented by the L E Fs.

On the negative side he speaks about those who have been false to the Reformation and have been slipshod in their preaching, having allowed it to become contemptible prose which no editorial writer even of a mediocre daily

paper would permit himself.[68] Such preaching
is, of course, the opposite of thought provoking.
In like manner, he speaks of the triumph of
disengagement and boredom as the result of
"Docetism" in modern preaching.

On the positive side, thought provoking
preaching is the result of (1) meeting the intellectual demands of preaching, (2) making the
Word contemporary, (3) speaking to men as
individuals, (4) engaging in "dialogue," (5)
helping men to ask the right questions, and (6)
of using the textual-thematic method.

Attention Holding—

Again we face the fact that to speak in such a
way as to hold attention is the result of much
that has been said under the previous headings.
However, ultimately the prime requirement for
attention holding preaching is for the preacher
to have something interesting to say. Thielicke
makes a point of this, but then adds that what
interests some members of a congregation may
not interest others.

Thielicke takes note of this problem of the
composition of his congregation and notes
especially that what interests the old ladies
of the congregation may not interest youth.
Above all the preacher dare not fall into the
trap of speaking for the most part only to the
old ladies. Although his comment reflects the
German church situation in particular, it is
relevant in principle to preaching everywhere.

He states flatly that the preacher "must speak for those who are not present *as if* they were present. This is a prescription which has been confirmed many times in practice."[69] He will gain the attention of those not present through those who report what has been proclaimed.

In other passages Thielicke describes the unfaithful witness, who, among other things, cannot hold the attention of his listeners. He explains why this is so.

> The unfaithful witness is the one who simply transmits the conventional and familiar, unchanged and undigested. He is unfaithful, in the first place, because he is lazy. For the labor of interpretation and contemporization, the work of "translation" is grueling work and it is never done without abortive trials and breath-taking risks.[70]

There is a price to be paid for effective preaching. Thielicke continues his description of the conventional preacher in the following paragraph:

> But the conventional preacher is unfaithful . . . because he gives his hearers stones instead of bread—venerable stones to be sure, but in this form they cannot be swallowed. And besides, in this way he travels the safest road so as to prevent any unpleasantnesses from arising. Nobody will ever get excited and so nobody will ever be excited against *him* either. . . . Boresomeness paralyzes people, but it does not make them an-

gry. And finally even the demons fall asleep.
But he who sleeps commits no sin, that is,
you don't flare up, you don't protest, you
never say "ouch," you don't say, "Crucify
him, let his blood be on us and on our children, I will have nothing to do with this
man." Nobody is ever shocked by lukewarm
drip from the pulpit, but that temperature
may make him sick enough to retch.[71]

With these and many other words he describes
the kind of innocuous preaching which not only
fails to hold the attention of the listener, but
betrays the Christian gospel.

Again, Thielicke would say that the cause
of much boredom and thus of lack of attention
is the "disaster of Docetism."[72]

Much might also be written about the relation of humor to interesting, attention holding
preaching. In this connection his discussion of
"cheerfulness" in the preaching of Spurgeon
and in Spurgeon's teaching of preaching is
worthy of attention for its own sake and because it shows Thielicke's interest in the subject. The following sentences indicate this
interest:

Spurgeon's humor is a mode of redemption because it is sanctified—because it grows
out of an overcoming of the world and therefore itself represents this overcoming of the
world in process. . . . Laughter is always
a form of engagement—of one type or another. If by nature I am a cheerful person
but there is not a sparkle of such cheerful-

ness in my preaching, it would amount to a dubious sign that in an essential part of my temperament I am still not really engaged by what I am saying.

When Spurgeon was cheerful and humorous in the pulpit, he was putting himself into his preaching; he was entering into the sermon with his whole nature. He who wants the interest of his hearers and wants them to be "in it" must first be in it himself.[73]

Thielicke then continues on his own with a guess on what Spurgeon might say today, were he to observe the modern church:

Should we not then, Spurgeon would probably ask in the face of the deadly seriousness with which the business of the church is pursued today, should we not see that lines of laughter about the eyes are just as much marks of faith as are the lines of care and seriousness? The church is in a bad way when it banishes laughter from the sanctuary and leaves it to cabaret, the night club, and the toastmasters.[74]

With the above sentence Thielicke leaves his discussion of "cheerfulness" in the preaching of Spurgeon, excepting to add the following sentence: "As important as humor in the *how* of preaching is having something interesting to say."[75] With this saying he evidently keeps humor in proper perspective. Nevertheless, when we read his comments on the place of humor in preaching, we are not surprised to discover that in his sermons there is inevitably some choice bit of humor that evokes a ripple of laughter or at least a chuckle throughout the congregation.

Finally, however, Thielicke is ever so much more interested in fulfilling the basic requirements of effective preaching, which is ultimately what holds the attention of the listeners.

Continuity—

The fourth major emphasis in Thielicke's discussion of "The Intellectual Demand of Preaching" is that preaching must be "ordered speech." That is to say, the sermon must be "clearly thought out and given a well-ordered structure. It must have movement, gradations, plateaus, and pauses."[76] This is fundamentally what we have treated as continuity in this study. "And when an unusually 'high' thought is introduced, it must be so embedded in the whole line of thought that the simple listener will not lose the thread."[77] All this, Thielicke reminds us, must be accomplished within a definite period of time counted in minutes.

As for his basic preaching method, we have already described his preference for *textual-thematic preaching*. Thielicke insists, as a general rule, on building a sermon around both a text and a central point in such a way that the central point is an outgrowth of the treatment of the text, and so that the central point enhances the text. This kind of preaching avoids the necessity of dealing with divergent elements in the text on the one hand and the faults of thematic preaching apart from a text on the other hand.[78]

Inspirational Quality—

After discussing the development of the text, the necessity of knowing his people, and the importance of "dialogue," Thielicke says:

> Then I must establish the contact between all this [all that he has learned from his people] and my text. And then I must express it in such a way that the intellect will be stimulated to think, the will mobilized, the conscience aroused, and the emotions engaged.[79]

We have shown that the layman defines inspirational quality as that which involves the listener emotionally as well as intellectually. It is that quality which "inspires" me to want to do what the preacher advocates or to accept what is offered in the message. This is what Thielicke is concerned with in the above quotation. He is also concerned with maintaining a balance in his approach, as we see in a succeeding passage.

> For after all, my message is one that concerns not only all men but also the *whole* man: the man of *feeling,* the man of intellect, the man of *will,* and the far larger contingent of those who are a mixture of all three. Must not the very focus and goal of my sermon be such that it addresses all of these dimensions?[80]

He goes on to relate his discussion to two important aspects of preaching: the question of the needs of the listeners and the requirement of love as a characteristic of the minister. Only when the latter is present can the minister feel the needs of the listeners. We might add that without this "love" it is not likely that the listener will be inspired toward Christian ends or goals. Thielicke concludes that without this love "all these ponderings of method and goals by which I seek to reach the conscience, feelings, will, and mental level of my hearers are good for nothing at all."[81]

Use of Illustrations—

In our sources Thielicke has little to say about the use of illustrations. There is one brief paragraph in *The Trouble with the Church* on how to interest young people in the sermon, which we might have quoted in relation to our discussion of attention holding, but did not do so. He describes the youth in the congregation with these words:

> There are the young people who still have their life before them. Some of them have already faced the question of the meaning of life. Others have minds that are stuffed with a melange of images garnered from television and the picture magazines. An "idea" would never catch them, at most perhaps a little story would.[82]

Although he goes on to speak of how he might

further interest the young people, he does not explain what kind of story he would tell them.

Thus, the way to get at how Thielicke makes use of illustrations is to study his use of them in his sermons and writings. Unquestionably, listeners agree that his use of illustrations is one of his distinctive characteristics, as will be shown in Chapter 7. His use of illustrations will also be noted in our special study of the sermon "The Cain Within Us," which makes up the second part of the present chapter.

The outstanding characteristic of Thielicke's use of illustrations is that they are chosen and told in such a way that it is possible for the listener to identify with the persons or action in the illustrations. His use of the story of the Canaanite woman is a case in point.[83] Thielicke's use of this little story has in it so many touches of human interest, humor, pathos, coupled with several original but quite legitimate applications that almost anyone would be fascinated with it. He concludes his two-page use of the story by saying:

> I imagine that this woman who was so unexpectedly healed continued to follow her Savior and that in further association with him she not only saw him from behind but also face to face, . . . And as she kept on following him, simply because she had been so puzzlingly and mysteriously accepted by him, she more and more grew out of her magical enthrallment and into a real discipleship.[84]

To be sure, Thielicke fills in certain details
out of his rich imagination. But all that he
writes is within the spirit of the account and
within the realm of probability. He applies the
story to life as follows:

> This would be growth, education, this
> would be meeting people where they are.
> This would be freedom to give oneself to
> people. This would be love. [It] should help
> us to grow out of our bondage to principles.[85]

Thielicke's use of this illustration, among
other uses, is an example of the use of an illustration for the purpose of *inspiration*. It should
inspire the listener to do what he suggests. In
the above discussion one is also aware of the
close relation between the *use of illustrations*
and *confrontation with decision*.

Preacher's Personality—

With regard to preacher's personality Edgar
Jackson writes:

> Preaching, whether or not we are willing
> to admit it, is essentially an art form, where
> a great idea is formed into artful expression
> through the impact of a competent person-
> ality upon an established medium.[86]

This concept of preaching stresses the role
of the preacher as the creator in the employ-
ment of an art form. His own personality is
then inseparably bound up with what is communicated.

Thielicke would undoubtedly agree that the

preacher's personality is inseparably bound up with what is communicated, but in *The Trouble with the Church,* he makes no direct observations about the relation of the personality of the preacher to preaching, and he most certainly says nothing about his personality as related to his preaching.

However, in *Encounter with Spurgeon* he lets Spurgeon speak for him about the preacher's personality in preaching. Following a passage in which he has raised the question as to how the minister should speak—should he speak in such a way as not to present himself and rather to retire behind the testimony and therefore present the sermon in a tone of aloof objectivity?—Thielicke answers in the words of Spurgeon:

> This is quite wrong. The fact is that the witness does not withdraw; he comes forward. (If he puts himself in the foreground like a prima donna and misuses the message merely as a means to play up himself, then this is something quite different and has absolutely nothing to do with what is meant here.) . . . Only as the witness himself comes forward will men regard him as credible and worth listening to.[87]

The words in parentheses are undoubtedly Thielicke's own words, his precaution against a misunderstanding. He continues:

> This coming forward of the witness, of course, need not by any means manifest it-

self in the use of the first person singular or
an autobiographical tone of speech. Nevertheless the individuality of the preacher
will undoubtedly make itself felt, or more
cautiously stated, dare not fight shy of letting itself be known.[88]

On the following page he seems to go even
farther, when he says:

The witness, however, discloses himself
in his own tone and individuality; for what
characterizes him is not only that he testi-
fies to *something,* but also that he is the one
who is testifying and "standing up" for it.[89]

These words would seem to characterize
Thielicke's practice as well as his principles.
From all the evidence it is clear that Thielicke
has the confidence that he is a chosen instrument in the hand of God and that he takes a
position of responsibility toward the message
he has to preach. Another point is also clear
to the writer, it is that Thielicke has no fear of
being "a personality," a person known for his
personal discipline in preparation, and a person who is not afraid to take a position on important issues.

He is determined that the quality of his
preaching shall not deteriorate. For example,
rather than to do an inferior (inferior by his
own standards) job of preaching at Michaelis
he would rather preach less often than former-
ly. Furthermore, he takes some pride in dealing
with difficult and delicate questions in his

preaching. At the present time he is preaching a series entitled "Jesus and the Crises in Our Lives." In 1966-67 he preached a series on the difficult question: "How Modern Dare Our Theology Be?"

Thielicke is also aware of occupying a unique position among preachers in respect to achieving a hearing by both liberals and conservatives theologically speaking. In fact he says as much:

> So people of all denominations and theological tendencies were apparently ready to listen to me. The liberals probably thought: He speaks in modern style, so he must be one of us; the Baptists said: He has written a book on Spurgeon, so he is close to us; the fundamentalists noted that my sermons were expositions of biblical texts and often included me in their ranks; and the Lutherans said: After all, he comes from Hamburg, ergo. . . .[90]

He also notes that he has been instrumental in getting diverse groups together in conversation. When the writer suggested that there are many Methodists who attend his services in St. Michaels, he stated that he was well aware of that fact and added that he has great appreciation for Methodists both in Germany and in the United States. Thielicke believes that his listening audience includes representatives of all denominations, including Roman Catholics, and people from all levels of society.

Thielicke is aware of being *a personality* in another sense. He knows that listeners are aware of his war-time record. He has not allowed them to forget about his disagreements with Nazi officials. His foreign journeys have been written-up and have been publicized through his accounts of them.

Previous to most of his major series of sermons, he has arranged a meeting with representatives of the religious and secular press in his university office in order to most effectively break the news of a new series. In these meetings a dozen persons are present, including his assistant (an assistant professor) and his secretary. Thielicke gives out just enough information on the nature of the series to come so that the newsmen can write an effective one or two column article, including a picture. He has been fortunate in that the secular press has given these releases prime front-page coverage. "Thielicke is news," said one informant. Just enough controversial material is included in the articles to make them interesting.

Thielicke is careful not to try to make himself to appear more important than he actually is; he does not claim to be a prophet or a "great one." One religious news editor told the writer that Thielicke does not claim to be a prophet; "he is too smart for that," he said. When asked whether Thielicke would think of himself as a prophet in the biblical sense as one who proclaims the will of God, this newsman agreed, "O yes! In that sense he both claims *to be* and *is* a prophet."

How does Thielicke think of himself? We conclude that his self-awareness includes the knowledge that he is a unique individual in the estimation of people and that in the providence of God he is an instrument of His will.

If we may assume that a man's commitment affects his personality and much of what he does, then it would seem to be pertinent to add here the following statement by Dr. Thielicke: "One thing I was always aware of: That man fails himself when he only seeks to find himself, and he only wins and realizes himself when he loses his life in God."[91]

Thus far nothing has been said here about Thielicke's personal appearance as a preacher. When he enters the chancel one notes immediately that he is a large, well-built man. He walks with dignity, but with a relatively relaxed movement of one who is accustomed to being observed. On closer observation one sees that he has an open, friendly, well-shaped face, which is capable of a wide range of expression. At fifty-nine years of age his head shows a considerable baldness.

When preaching at St. Michaels in Hamburg he wears the customary Lutheran robe and flared collar. He preaches with great intensity during much of the hour-long delivery of the sermon. A number of the interviewees called attention to the fact that he repeatedly takes a handkerchief from his pocket to wipe the perspiration from his forehead. Some said that he has in the past used relays of handkerchiefs, but the writer saw no evidence of this. He did use one handkerchief a number of times, as unobtrusively as possible, considering the summer heat, the humidity, and his rather wide expanse of forehead.

Thielicke has a relatively deep bass speaking voice which he uses to good advantage. He speaks in a tone of voice with an exceptionally high degree of naturalness. Even when he expands the volume of tone there is no undesirable change of quality. He has mastered the art of public speech far beyond the average minister. This undoubtedly contributes to his success.

Manner of Delivery—

Actually, we have already been discussing Thielicke's manner of delivery in relation to his use of his voice, and in the comment on the intensity with which he speaks. We have yet to discuss his ideals and practice as related to style of delivery, use of words, fluency, and other related matters.

Although one should never conclude that Thielicke is against striving for rhetorical and pedagogical excellence, we must emphasize that these are never his first concern. He is most concerned to speak to real men in their need in such a way that the resources of the gospel are brought to bear on those needs. Nevertheless, Thielicke believes that when we delve deeply into the causes of the crisis in preaching we come up with the problems of the language used in preaching.

He has no use for what he calls "grasping for surprise effects in church life . . . the desperate recourse to shocking, offensive, coarse, or hyper-modern words. . . ."[92] We have an account of his ridiculing of the preacher who turned on the rhetorical explosions in order to dispel the boredom by pseudodramatizations.[93] Moreover, it is in relation to the language of preaching that he says preaching becomes incredible and hollow when it simply employs the conventional vocabulary without reworking it.

Thielicke insists that we must use words which actually make our theology understandable. He introduces a word of caution when he cites Martin Kahler as indicating that

> There is such a thing as accommodation motivated by love which seeks to reach the other person by speaking his language, and that alongside of it there may be an accommodation motivated by opportunism which simply agrees with what others say and tells them only what they want to hear.[94]

Nevertheless, in general Thielicke concludes that the more a man speaks in modern terms, the more he will be heard.[95]

Thielicke notes that Spurgeon puts the physical side of speech, including voice culture and gestures, into proper perspective when he says these are not merely a matter of the rules and techniques of rhetoric to be learned for their own sake, but are a part of the service which the speaker must render to the Word and its utterance, the service which he is supposed to perform in love for the neighbor to whom he owes the Word.[96] This again does not mean that he scorns rhetoric. Speaking of Thielicke, one need only to hear him preach to be convinced that he has paid minute attention to the details of rhetoric. It would be reemphasized that his early training as well as his inclinations from the time of early youth make this part of his effort not necessarily routine but something which he expects of himself.

Prophetic Voice—

Thielicke spends little time and effort in talking about what a modern prophet should do, unless one would broaden the concept "prophet" to make it synonymous with minister or with preacher. In our lay-definition of what it means to be a prophetic voice the emphasis is laid on the answers to the following questions: Does he have a message for our time? Does he call us to repentance? Is he a modern Amos or a Jeremiah? What does he have to say about the great problems of our time? The latter question includes problems of community, nation, and of the church. In this sense, is Thielicke a prophet? Does he speak with a prophetic voice?

In pleading with ministers to proclaim the word and in denouncing them for their flight into liturgism, he speaks like a prophet. In criticizing the national church for its failings he speaks like a prophet. When he raises questions about baptism, confirmation and general church practices he is speaking like a prophet. He does not predict, for example, when he questions certain developments in the ecumenical movement, but he warns and states his reservations as would a prophet. As the prophets suffered for criticizing the establishment of their times, Thielicke suffers for daring to criticize time-worn customs of the church.

On the national scene Thielicke is even now under severe criticism for his views. His consistently anti-communist position (right or wrong) has cost him the respect of some who would take a more conciliatory or a more mediatory position.

Whether his new posture on the use of modern theology in preaching as developed in the booklet containing the four sermons on the general subject of *How Modern Dare Our Theology Be?* is prophetic we must leave to the reader to judge. The writer heard a considerable amount of criticism on the series at the 1967 Kirchentag. The conservative view is that Thielicke has gone much too far in recognizing the contributions of the "new theology." The majority

view, however, is that it was high time that a
capable, informed, and recognized scholar of
Thielicke's caliber came out into the open and
let the people in on what the theologians are
thinking, believing and teaching. Thielicke
was only doing in the series at the Kirchentag
what he had already done in 1966 at Michaelis,
and what he had long been doing in his lectures
at the University of Hamburg.[97]

Perhaps Thielicke is as near being a prophetic voice when he reminds his hearers that they
must reckon with God—as near as at any other
time. Rudolf Michael, an editorial writer of the
newspaper "Bild am Sonntag," writes in this
popular Sunday paper, quoting Thielicke,

> God is only near me when I know . . . that
> he has come to me on my street . . . Before
> God everything will become quiet . . . the
> noisy miracles of the economic world, the
> political fears, the heated confrontations,
> the spectres of bombs and rockets.[98]

At this point the writer of the article adds,
"Thielicke storms [thunders] against making
a God out of work."

Basis and Use of Authority—

Thielicke expresses his views emphatically
on the question of the basis and source of the
preacher's authority. After putting together for
his readers all of the main ingredients of what
he calls "The Intellectual Demand of Preaching," he surveys what he has written and re-

acts to it as follows:

> Where is the man who can accomplish all
> this and who among those who are faced
> with this enormous assignment does not
> despair of accomplishing it? . . . The only
> man who can assume such a bold and haz-
> ardous task is one who is convinced that he
> need not bear the responsibility for its suc-
> cess and that Another is there interceding
> for him. He knows that not he but only the
> Spirit of God himself is able to reach and
> open the hearts of his hearers.[99]

Here we have not only the *basis of authority,*
but an emphasis on the need for dependence
on "Another," dependence on the Spirit of God.
Thielicke believes that only to the degree that
the preacher is assured of all this will he
mount the pulpit consoled and strengthened.
He reminds us that "even this faith in the miracle of the Spirit can be secured only through
practice. It can become a deep, sustaining power
only by the exercise of prayer and through
one's own listening to the message of the text
which is being preached."[100]
Although Thielicke clearly does not hold to
a "verbal inspiration" theory, he nevertheless
has an implicit faith in the efficacy of "listening to the message of the text." Although the
Bible can be subjected to the scrutiny of critical
scholarship it is, nevertheless, authoritative
for preaching. Thielicke speaks of those who
listened to the lectures of Spurgeon as living in

the atmosphere of the Bible. "They no longer needed to be exhorted to take the Bible seriously; it penetrated into what the psychologists call the 'image level' of their unconscious."[101] When one hears Thielicke preach or reads his sermons, one feels that his relationship to the Bible is something akin to what he has described in Spurgeon's listeners.

What about Thielicke's use of authorities outside of the Bible? In every sermon he preaches he quotes from a number of authorities such as: the church fathers, biblical scholars, poets, philosophers, and even secular authorities as suits his purposes. His foremost and most often used authority is Martin Luther.

Does he speak as if he himself is an authority whom the listener must recognize? If it is a question as to whether he speaks authoritatively, one must answer "yes." If, however, we ask whether he imposes *himself* into a discussion as an authority, then one must answer that the listener is seldom aware of the feeling that this is happening. This stems not so much from a lack of pronouncements or from a lack of positive assertions in his preaching, but from the fact that Thielicke seldom interjects the personal pronoun "I" into such assertions. Table 3 on Page 204 summarizes his use of pronouns in one sermon. This table indicates how he takes his congregation along with him by his use of the personal pronouns "we," "us," and "you," in many of his assertions. This is no way diminishes the necessity for, nor the fact that he takes one along with him by his logical development of the sermon.

Evidence of Preparation—

When one listens to a sermon by Thielicke, the prime evidence of preparation is, of course, the message itself. Secondly, although it is obvious to everyone that he takes his multiple-page manuscript into the pulpit with him, and although he turns the pages regularly as he progresses in the delivery of the sermon, he presents it in such a way that he appears not to be reading, but speaks in highly personal conversational tones, fluently, and with a wide variation of tonal inflections. A comparison of a printed sermon with a recording of the same sermon reveals that there is considerable difference in terminology and sentence structure but very little difference in the continuity and the basic content of the sermon. This indicates that Thielicke trusts his memory or his mind to reproduce what he has on the typed page without the necessity of following it word for word. This also means that his preparation goes far beyond the composition of the message. He says that he often dictates his message to a "recording machine" in preparation for its presentation.

In preparation for the delivery of sermons in America he, with the help of his interpreter, practiced speaking his translated manuscripts

to the point where he could speak the correct
pronunciations and even the correct inflections
in English. Dr. Darrell Guder, who assisted
him, has said that Thielicke was indefatigable
in this accomplishment.

There is another aspect of sermon preparation
about which Thielicke speaks in this way:

> The preparation of a sermon requires a
> continuing exercise of an inner, spiritual
> order. And above all it requires an exercise,
> a training in love, and hence a work (yes, a
> "work") which includes the whole man.[102]

This area of preparation has to do not only
with what he does in his study, and in his devo-
tional life, but also with all his relationships.
Thielicke writes as follows about what this
means:

> He must really settle a rift in his marriage,
> a loss of trust in relationship to his children,
> the bad situation with his fellow minister,
> and he must learn to carry out this loving
> understanding existentially in order not
> to contradict himself and remain convincing,
> indeed, in order to be able to reach his hear-
> ers at all.[103]

At this point Thielicke cites what he has
written in *Encounter With Spurgeon* on this
subject. There he puts into one complex sentence what it means to prepare for preaching:

> Preaching encompasses a tremendously
> broad complex of procedures—ranging from

prayer for the miracle of the Spirit through study of the text itself and the structuring of a sermon outline to the workmanlike mastery of effective speech—real standards can be found only in living examples.[104]

In the last line above he refers to the reading of sermons by great preachers of the past as a means of *preparation.*

In encouraging the reader to study the sermons of Spurgeon he takes a verbal whack at the overemphasis on hermeneutics, when he says:

It would only indicate that we had been driven mad by the art of hermeneutics if we were no longer capable of accepting and valuing, as a corrective of our perfect exegesis, the childlike candor of a preacher who could "listen like a disciple."[105]

The corrective, Thielicke says, is charismatic listening. He refers to listening to the text of the scriptures chosen as central to the development of the sermon. We should add to preparation Thielicke's emphasis on "dialogue," and in listening to the laymen.

Thielicke writes of the ability of Spurgeon to give thematic titles to his sermons that challenge our curiosity and interest, such as "The Golden Muzzle" (on Acts 4:14) or the mysterious sounding "Perhaps" (on Zeph. 2:3).[106] This is an area of preparation to which Thielicke gives much attention as we may realize from a study of the sermon titles used in his published sermons.

One aspect of preparation cannot be over-emphasized. This Thielicke teaches by example and by word of testimony. When we consider the amount of study, the labor and pain that has gone into the preparation for preaching of the sermons of Thielicke, then we are prepared to accept his statement that "the discipline and the hard application must be taken care of before the witness begins to speak."[107]

There is a sense in which preparation encompasses all of the characteristics of preaching emphasized as important by laymen. When the total *preparation* effort, including *prayer-preparation, charismatic listening,* the *structuring* of the sermon, the detailed work on the *language,* the choice of *illustrations,* and the work on the *content* of the sermon as a whole is inadequate, the quality of the preaching suffers whether or not the preacher or his people are aware of their loss. Ultimately the congregation shares the responsibility for maintaining the quality of the preaching by its standard of expectation; by its standard of expectation it supports the minister in the discipline necessary for preparation.

When we speak of *evidence of preparation,* this is something which each listener will measure by his own standards. Many German listeners prefer not to think about the sermon in terms of evidence of preparation. And for the minister to give evidence of preparation is obviously a secondary incentive. But for the layman a sermon which gives little evidence of preparation will also provide little incentive, especially for the prospect of enduring another similar sermon. From this point of view Thielicke's scorn for ministers who are "lazy" is understandable and forgivable.[108]

Love - Fear (Quality of Motivation)—

Thielicke's fear of psychologizing and his desire for genuineness in his feelings and motives may tend to prevent him from having much to say about the subject of motivation in and through the sermon. This is understandable. He does raise questions as to his own inner motivation. He asks whether the love which is so indispensable to preaching is always at his command? And he expects his reader to raise this question about his own attitude? He realizes that the basic attitudes of the minister are apt to come through to the listener regardless of what the words used express; we have already shown this in our discussion of credibility. He says:

> After all, I too have my fits of rage over the blaring portable in my neighbor's garden, I too have my moments of depression and feelings of envy, and often my heart is so glutted with them that there is hardly any room left in the inn of the inner man for love and loving understanding of others.

> But then all these ponderings of method and
> goals by which I seek to reach the conscience,
> feelings, will, and mental level of my hear-
> ers are good for nothing at all. For without
> love, everything I say, no matter how in-
> geniously worked out it may be, becomes a
> noisy gong and a clanging cymbal.[109]

We have looked at this question before, both
in relation to credibility and in relation to
inspirational quality. But should we not again
ask the question: will not my basic attitude be
felt in what I say and the way I say it, whether
I speak of joy or pain, pleasure or anxiety, love
or hate, heaven or hell? Is not the basic question, after all, whether the minister reaches out
to men in love? Or, does he seem to want to
somehow force them, by all his use of techniques
and methods, to do what he advocates for reasons not founded in love? Thielicke writes:

> All our Christian sovereignty over our
> multiple motives and all our childlike trust
> in him who knows our hearts and will be a
> merciful judge obviously cannot exempt us
> from the task of searching our hearts and
> facing the self-critical question of where
> the real center of our motives lies.[110]

We have every reason to believe that Thielicke does subject his heart to this kind of self-
scrutiny. What happens as a result of all his
soul-searching in regard to his use of the motivational elements represented by the *love - fear*
polarities of this lay expectation factor in his

effort to motivate listeners will be seen in the analysis of the sermon in Part II of this chapter and in the report in Chapter 7 on the evaluation of the laymen of his use of these motivational qualities.

Originality—

Judging by all the evidence available in our study of L E Fs in the preaching of Helmut Thielicke, *originality* is one of the characteristics peculiarly strong in that preaching as compared to its strength in the preaching of Woldemar Lein. When we study his printed sermons we find this characteristic is present in most of them. Thielicke listeners as a rule have felt that he is more original in his preaching than other preachers they have heard. It is quite certain that Thielicke's preaching has a degree of originality not often experienced in the work of other preachers.

However, when we search his writings on preaching, we do not so much as hear him use the word "originality," or as used in German, *Originalität.*

We hear him warn against simply transmitting the conventional and the familiar, unchanged and undigested. We hear him speak of the necessity of interpretation and contemporization, of preaching so that the Word becomes flesh again, so that it enters into our own time, wearing the dress of the present; all of which, in a comparative sense, may imply originality, but we never hear him say "be original."

Nevertheless, Thielicke is an original thinker and his sermons are filled with examples of this characteristic. He would probably not want to be original just for the sake of being original, particularly not in preaching, which must bear the stamp of authenticity. But when it comes to interpretation and contemporization of the meaning of scripture, there he becomes original in order to carry out his obligation and intention as a preacher.

Range of Subjects—

Here again, we learn from Thielicke largely by studying his example. We may study his selection of Bible texts; we may make note of which books of the Bible he uses most. We have noted that he returns again and again to certain central themes like the "Prodigal Son," and "Love for the Neighbor." The essential task is to preach on the essential texts and to deal with the subjects which demand attention in our time.

NOTES AND REFERENCES

[1]Helmut Thielicke, *The Trouble With the Church* (New York: Harper and Row, Publishers, 1965).

[2]H. T., *Encounter with Spurgeon* (Philadelphia: Fortress Press, 1963).

[3]*The Trouble With the Church, op. cit.,* p. 1.

[4]*Ibid.,* p. 3.

[5]*Ibid.*

[6]*Ibid.,* p. 2.

[7]Irving J. Lee, "Four Ways of Looking at a Speech" (*The Quarterly Journal of Speech,* XXVIII, April, 1942), p. 153.

[8]Roger Brown, *Words and Things* (Glencoe, Illinois: The Free Press, 1958), p. 307.

[9]*The Trouble With the Church, op. cit.,* p. 11.

[10]*Ibid.,* p. 14.

[11]*Ibid.,* p. 5.

[12]*Ibid.*

[13]*Ibid.,* p. 10.

[14]*Ibid.,* p. 15.

[15]*Ibid.*

[16]*Ibid.,* p. 13.

[17]*Ibid.,* p. 15.

[18]*Encounter With Spurgeon, op. cit.,* p. 22.

[19]*Ibid.*

[20]*The Trouble With the Church, op. cit.,* p. 18.

[21]*Ibid.,* p. 16.

[22]*Ibid.,* p. 17.

[23]*Ibid.,* p. 19.

[24] *The Trouble With the Church, op. cit.,* p. 21.

[25]*Ibid.*

[26]*Ibid.,* p. 22.

[27]*Ibid.,* p. 23.

[28]*Ibid.,* p. 20.

[29]*Ibid.*

[30]*Ibid.*

[31]*Ibid.,* p. 21.

[32]*Ibid.,* p. 25.

[33]*Ibid.,* p. 43.

[34]*Ibid.,* p. 63.

[35]*Ibid.,* p. 64.

[36]*Ibid.*, p. 98.

[37]*Ibid.*, p. 25.

[38]*Ibid.*, p. 26.

[39]*Ibid.*, p. 27.

[40]*Ibid.*, p. 29.

[41]*Ibid.*, p. 30.

[42]*Ibid.*, see pp. 35, 36.

[43]*Ibid.*, p. 36.

[44]*Ibid.*, p. 40.

[45]*Ibid.*, p. 50.

[46]*Ibid.*, p. 76.

[47]*Ibid.*, p. 67.

[48]*Ibid.*, p. 68.

[49]*Ibid.*

[50]*Ibid.*, p. 77.

[51]In this connection see page 77.

[52]*The Trouble With the Church, op. cit.*, p. 74.

[53]*Ibid.*, p. 75.

[54]*Ibid.*, p. 84.

[55]*Ibid.*, p. 97.

[56]*Ibid.*

[57]*Ibid.*, p. 128.

[58]*Ibid.*, p. 130.

[59]*Ibid.*, p. 22.

[60]*Ibid.*, p. 55.

[61]*Ibid.*

[62]*Ibid.*, p. 115.

[63]*Ibid.*

[64]*Ibid.*, p. 116.

[65]*Ibid.*, p. 117.

[66]*Ibid.*, pp. 117, 118.

[67]H. T., *Auf Kanzel und Katheder,* p. 131 [Trans. m. d.].

[68]*The Trouble With the Church, op. cit.,* 105.

[69]*Ibid.*, p. 32.

[70]*Ibid.*, p. 40.

[71]*Ibid.*

[72]*Ibid.*, p. 77.

[73]*Encounter With Spurgeon, op. cit.*, p. 25.

[74]*Ibid.*, p. 26.

[75]*Ibid.*

[76]*The Trouble With the Church, op. cit.*, p. 24.

[77]*Ibid.*

[78]*Ibid.*, pp. 61-65. Supra, pp. 152-155.

[79]*Ibid.*, p. 22.

[80]*Ibid.*

[81]*Ibid.*, p. 23.

[82]*Ibid.*, p. 21.

[83]*Ibid.*, p. 92.

[84]*Ibid.*, p. 93.

[85]*Ibid.*

[86]Edgar Jackson, *A Psychology for Preaching* (Great Neck, New York: Channel Press, Inc., 1961), p. 60.

[87]*Encounter With Spurgeon, op. cit.*, pp. 37, 38.

[88]*Ibid.*, p. 38.

[89]*Ibid.*, p. 39.

[90]H. T., *Between Heaven and Earth* (New York: Harper & Row, Publishers, 1965), p. xiv, [see preface].

[91]H. T., *Auf Kanzel und Katheder*, p. 16.

[92]*The Trouble With the Church, op. cit.*, p. 47.

[93]*Ibid.*, p. 43.

[94]*Ibid.*, p. 39.

[95]See the discussion of this question in connection with "theological content" on pp. 155-159.

[96]*Encounter With Spurgeon, op. cit.*, p. 15.

[97]For discussion of the above series, see pp. 130-135.

[98]"Bild am Sonntag," (Hamburg: December 14, 1958), p. 14.

[99] *The Trouble With the Church, op. cit.,* pp. 24, 25.
[100] *Ibid.,* p. 25.
[101] *Encounter With Spurgeon, op. cit.,* p. 9.
[102] *The Trouble With the World, op. cit.,* p. 24.
[103] *Ibid.,* p. 24.
[104] *Encounter With Spurgeon, op. cit.,* p. 2.
[105] *Ibid.,* p. 3.
[106] *Ibid.,* p. 26.
[107] *Ibid.,* p. 40.
[108] *The Trouble With the Church, op. cit.,* p. 40.
[109] *Ibid.,* p. 23.
[110] *Ibid.,* p. 83.

Chapter 6

A SERMON ANALYSIS

The sermon to be analyzed is entitled "The Cain Within Us." It is sermon Number 13, from the book of sermons published in Philadelphia, Pa., by Muhlenberg Press, in 1961, under the title *How the World Began.* This series of sermons was translated by John W. Doberstein from Thielicke's *Wie die Welt Begann; der Mensch in der Urgeschichte der Bibel,* Stuttgart: Quell-Verlag, 1960.

The series of sermons of which this sermon is a part was introduced and discussed briefly beginning on page 114 in our Chapter 4. The series was preached by Thielicke at Michaelis beginning in 1957 and continuing through 1959. This particular sermon was chosen for analysis because it was thought to illustrate how Thielicke meets the requirements of preaching as expressed by laymen in terms of *lay expectation factors.* Also, it was preached near the mid-point of Thielicke's ministry at Michaelis. Otherwise it is probably no more typical of his preaching than any one of a hundred or more of his sermons might be said to be typical.

Our method will be to record the words of the sermon at the top of the page and to record the analysis of the sermon in the space below the line near the middle of the page. Each mention of an L E F will be underlined. Other key words relating the analysis to the apparatus of speech, homiletics, or to the terms of the present study will also be underlined.

THE CAIN WITHIN US

The Story of Cain and Abel: Part One

Now Adam knew Eve his wife, and she conceived and bore Cain, saying, "I have gotten a man with the help of the Lord." And again, she bore his brother Abel. Now Abel was a keeper of sheep, and Cain a tiller of the ground. In the course of time Cain brought to the Lord an offering of the fruit of the ground, and Abel brought of the firstlings of his flock and of their fat portions. And the Lord had regard for Abel and his offering, but for Cain and his offering he had no regard. So Cain was very angry, and his countenance fell. The Lord said to Cain, "Why are you angry, and why has your countenance fallen? If you do well, will you not be accepted? And if you do not do well, sin is crouching at the door; its desire is for you, but you must master it."

Cain said to Abel his brother, "Let us go out to the field." And when they were in the field, Cain rose up against his brother Abel, and killed him.

—Genesis 4:1-8

The sound and healthy world of creation now lies behind man. The cherub with the flaming, slashing sword sees to it that there is no returning. The logic of events which follow from one great, initial wrong decision goes on ineluctably working itself out.

The introductory words of this sermon help to bridge the gap between the previous sermons in the series and the sermon just beginning. The previous sermon was entitled "The Mystery of Death"; it centered on the account of the expulsion of Adam and Eve from the Garden of Eden. Thielicke captures the *attention* of his audience by plunging into the drama of the expulsion of Adam and Eve from the Garden of Eden. In so doing he summarizes the background leading to the text which has just been read. The story is retold simply, without reference to historical criticism or hermeneutical method. "The logic of events which follow from one great, initial wrong, etc." was probably intended to relate the sermon to contemporary events in Germany as well as to events of the past, events only too well known to many of the people assembled before Thielicke. His very first sentence, "The sound and healthy world of creation now lies behind man," reminds his listeners of the unsound and in many ways unhealthy world in which they live.

The word "ineluctably" is a translation of a well-understood German word (*zwangsläufig*) meaning "as if forced to keep running" or very near our word "inevitably." Thielicke shows how one event leads to another. The factor of *relevance* in this sermon emerges with the first short sentences in the introduction. Thielicke's introduction is an introduction to the actual sermon, not as so many other introduc-

From the plucking of the forbidden fruit there now develops Cain's fratricide, and already the first stones of the tower of Babel are being gathered together.

What now commences—at precisely the point which marks the boundary of the intact world and closes it off to the rear—we call "world history." It is the space into which we are "thrown;" the space in which Cain lifts his ax and Abel falls lifeless to the ground: the space in which creatures fight to the death for a place in the sun, in which the stronger triumph and right is threatened by power; the space in which according to Goethe, the battle between belief and unbelief is fought out and in which the miracle men of history, the "world-historical individuals" rise from the abyss to "conquer half the globe" and then fall back again into the depths from which they came.

---

tions which are introductions to the sermon hour. His introduction is *relevant* to the purpose of the sermon.

Thielicke is a master of the use of *contrast* and *comparison.* Already in the introduction, the members of his congregation by comparing and contrasting their world to the world of the past to which there is no returning, are caused to relate to the words of the preacher. World history is something that has been going on for a long time. We are "thrown" into it; we cannot avoid it. Thielicke is a master of *description;* how vividly he describes our world.

The second paragraph contains his first reference to an outside *authority.* The words he

The history of the world is the space in which Cain's ax finally becomes dynamite and phosphorus, hydrogen explosions and space rockets.

One must pay very careful attention in order to catch the precise second in which world history began to unfold. This initial impulse, the direction the first movement takes will determine the curve of all future events. This terse, age-old story of Cain and Abel is the pattern for everything that we can see in ourselves and all around us. He that is able to find the key to this extremely concentrated extract of history will find that nothing human and also nothing divine is any longer alien to him.

---

selects from Goethe supplement his own words when he speaks of "world-historical individuals" who rise from the abyss to "conquer half the globe" and then fall back into the depths from which they came.

He becomes even more *relevant* and *contemporary* when he says, "The history of the world is the space where Cain's ax finally becomes dynamite and phosphorus, hydrogen explosions and space rockets."[23]

His way of using the Bible—relating the Bible to history and explaining history by the Bible is illustrated here especially in the sentence, "This terse, age-old story of Cain and Abel is the pattern for everything, etc." He speaks of the "key" to be found in this extremely concentrated extract of history, with which he leads his hearer to expect to understand the secrets of sacred and secular, the human and the di-

Therefore we must proceed with utmost caution. As in the case of the story of the Fall, we shall not be able to dispose of it in one onslaught and we shall have to make several attempts to find a path through the primitive rock of the story of Cain and Abel. But once we have traversed this massif, we shall know ourselves better than before and more easily find our way through the terrain of our own lives.

If you read the story of Cain and Abel only half way through, you expose yourself to a shock. For, without any reason being given, we are suddenly and abruptly told that "the Lord had regard for Abel and his offering, but for Cain and his offering he had no regard." We search in vain for what the

---

vine—with these words he heightens the expectation of the listener, and at the same time explains his *theology*.

In a further *introductory* or possibly *transitional* paragraph Thielicke seems to be trying to inject a feeling of caution, or of mystery, in order to raise the expectation of his listeners. For he says, "We shall have to make several attempts to find a path through the primitive rock of the story of Cain and Abel."

Thielicke emphasizes all of the *thought provoking* aspects of the story. For example, "We are suddenly and abruptly told that 'the Lord had regard for Abel and his offering, but for Cain. . . he had no regard.'" He builds up suspense as he struggles with this thought; he *asks questions* which he does not immediately answer. He makes his listeners do some thinking

lawyers call a "basis for judgment." There must be
some reason, some motive for God's strange reaction of approval of Abel and rejection of Cain! Was
Abel perhaps a highly moral and religious man?
Was Cain a questionable character, a secret rebel?

Perhaps, but we are not directly told that this is
so. We have only this account written in the tersest
telegram style. Only the skeleton of events is indicated and this bony structure is not clothed with
even a modicum of narrative flesh, much less a fatty
deposit of epic breadth. And search as we may in
this archaically spare account for clues which might
explain God's attitude, we find none at all at first,
for everything said of both the brothers seems to
be run on precisely parallel lines.

Both come from the same parents, and thus have,
to express it in modern terms, the same heredity.
Both pursue a solid, steady, we might say, elemental, vocation: the one is a farmer, the other a shepherd. Both approach an altar and perform a religious
act of worship. One may also assume—though this
is not explicitly stated—that each of them brought
the choicest offerings from their own spheres of
work, Abel the best sheep of his flock and Cain the
richest fruit of his harvest.

---

on their own. He stresses the "telegram style"
of the account, as if to say, "You see, one has to
fill in the details." He draws *parallels* and *contrasts* as he describes what is known about the
brothers.

Thielicke does not say it, but we are certain
that he is causing his listeners to raise the
question: Why do we become the persons we

But all this is only suggested by dotted lines and is not emphasized. It is only the overture to the first scene we see when the curtain actually rises: the one is accepted and the other rejected. Abel departs with a blessing. But Cain's countenance falls and he begins to brood and devise mischief.

At the altar of God, in the midst of devout worship, the threads of fate become entangled in the first knots, and the process never ceased until nets and snares were formed. Later on it will be said concerning the end of history that judgment will "begin with the household of God" (1 Pet. 4:17). The unfaithful church and the idolatrous altars, from which curse instead of blessing, confusion instead of salvation has gone forth, will be the *first* to be visited by the wrathful judgments of God.

---

know ourselves to be? Why am I like I am? Thielicke's explanations have several results: For some listeners the story will become more comprehensible; for others more *thought provoking questions* are raised.

But all this is only "overture" to the first scene . . . (and also for the sermon) the one is accepted and the other rejected—the incredible shock.

The next paragraph is a deeply *theological* passage. Thielicke for the first time in the sermon quotes from the New Testament: "Later on it will be said concerning the end of history that judgment will 'begin with the household of God.'" Thielicke cites the exact scripture reference. Here we see his *concern for the church,*

Anybody who has any instinct at all for what is weird and uncanny senses that something appalling is being said in this ballad of Cain and Abel and that here allusions are being made to the deep hinterlands of the world. There is the sound of some dark strain here which we must pursue and examine.

In the first place in any case, when we think of

---

when he speaks of "the unfaithful church and the idolatrous altars, . . . etc." The writer is convinced that Thielicke's *concern for the church* is genuine and that it is evident in his sermons. However, as in this passage, in this context, and because of the suggestion of judgment on the "church and the idolatrous altars from which curse instead of blessing, etc." the layman may miss the fact of concern for the church. To be sure, the note of judgment is strong in this passage. Thielicke occasionally bears down on the side of the *fear-anxiety* elements in his desire to motivate. He does not preach only *love* and *forgiveness*. There is a balance in what in this study we have called the *love-fear* (motivation) factor.

Here Thielicke will catch the ear of the student, of the skeptic, of the liberal, when he says, "Anybody who has any instinct for what is weird and uncanny senses that something appalling . . . in this ballad of Cain and Abel. . . ." He calls it a ballad, but only in passing. "There is a sound of some dark strain . . ."—more mystery, more *attention holding, thought provoking,* and highly *descriptive* wording.

the absence of any basis for God's judgment, we
are faced with the question whether everything
depends on whether a person happens to suit or not
to suit God. Was there some reason why Cain did
not "suit" God?

There is a voice within us which is inclined to
agree with this melancholy question. After all,
don't we see it being confirmed all around us in life?

There are people who are good and decent in their
way, but they have no luck. In examinations they
get the very question for which they are not prepared. When they drive a car they are always hit-
ting the red lights. And of all the nice girls they
meet, they always get stuck with "plain Jane." They
are always out of luck. Could this be the type that
does not suit God whom he allows to flounder
about?

He is back where three minutes before, he
asked the question, "Was Cain a secret rebel?"
Only this time in his *rephrasing* of the *thought
provoking* question, he asks, "Was there some
reason why Cain did not suit God?"

The question becomes *contemporary:* "Don't
we see it confirmed all around us in life?" The
listener knows that this is the place where
Thielicke will bring us a series of *specific instances* of the kind in which people make ex-
cuses for their actions in terms of "bad luck,"
like getting caught by "changing lights," or by
failing the one exam "question they had not
studied," and one *example* which Doberstein
either missed or purposely mistranslated, when
Thielicke says, "And of all the nice girls they

And then again there are other people for whom everything runs smoothly. Their children get only A's in school, they never have to go to the dentist, and all they have to do is smile and everything falls into their laps. Apparently they are the good Lord's Sunday children who suit him very well. "For some are in the dark and the others in the light." *The Three-penny Opera* has plenty to say about this sad way of dividing things up.

---

meet, they had to catch the one 'bad Hilde'." Doberstein's "plain Jane" completely misses the point. It was a point not missed by his German hearers, the kind of point which probably caused a mild twitter of laughter or probably a few guffaws. This is an example of the kind of language to which Klaus Juhl objects in his critique of Thielicke. It is a part of his *cheerfulness,* and in terms of Spurgeon, of his *worldliness* or even *earthiness.* Perhaps it only used to jerk to *attention* some of the young people in the congregation. At the same time, the "bad girl" example may make the point he is striving for at the moment. Someone may say to himself, so this is why my luck is like Cain's? Thielicke asks, "Could this be the type that does not suit God and whom he allows to flounder about?" In this humorous but *thought provoking manner* Thielicke proceeds with additional *Illustrations,* including that "The Three-penny Opera has plenty to say about this sad way of dividing things up."

But is this really all the Bible has to say about the freedom of God, the freedom which supposedly permits him to do as he pleases and thus indirectly suggests that God is merely capricious? Do the manger in Bethlehem and the cross on Golgotha, do the Lord's Prayer and the Lord's high-priestly prayer really have nothing more to proclaim than this one hard, distressing fact that God can do what he wills, that he chooses Abel as his favorite and has a grudge against Cain? This is hardly possible. But then what is the case?

A first bit of light upon the mystery of this strange circumstance may lie in the fact that the names Cain and Abel have meanings which are revealing. Cain means "I have gotten a man." Thus Eve, the proud mother, suggests that this son will bear the dignity of being the first-born and that for her he is to be the quintessence of power and strength.

With a question, "But is this all the Bible has to say about the freedom of God, . . ." Thielicke has returned to his central question: Can God do whatever he wills, and how is this related to God's freedom? Thielicke literally spoofs the suggestion and asks the *biblically* and *theologically   relevant* question: "Do   the manger, . . . the cross, . . . the Lord's Prayer and the Lord's high-priestly prayer really have nothing more to proclaim . . . than that God can do what he wills, that he chooses Abel as his favorite and has a grudge against Cain?"

Here Thielicke introduces a somewhat *original* thought; at least it will seem to be original for many listeners. He dwells on the meaning

Abel on the other hand means something like "nothingness, frailty." The younger brother is thus overshadowed by the elder from the very beginning. He is destined to play second fiddle. He is the represenitive of those who get the short end of the stick. He is the typical *déclassé*.

Everything that subsequently builds up into dramatic tension and finally explodes in the catastrophe of fratricide ultimately derives from this inequality of the roles in which Cain and Abel and all others find themselves: the fact that some have favorable chances to begin with and like Cain are provided with the privileges of the first-born, whereas others grow up in the shadows and are nobodies.

Did Eve do right in thus determining the unequal

---

of the names: Cain and Abel; Cain "is to be the quintessence of power and strength," while— and here Thielicke draws another sharp *contrast*—Abel is the typical *déclassé*. Thielicke occasionally uses a French or an English word, if it will serve his purpose. The word *déclassé* was understood by most of his listeners. At any rate, the next paragraph would help to explain it.

In a powerful sentence he then brings the ancient story and the present day together, when he says, "Everything that subsequently builds up into dramatic tension and finally explodes in the catastrophe of fratricide ultimately derives from this *inequality of the roles* in which Cain and Abel and *all others* find themselves: . . ." He then asks the *thought provok-*

destiny of these two in the very cradle by showing
favoritism and discrimination? Well, the fact is
that now Eve is acting outside of paradise; she is
the mother of world-history—and, after all, this is
the way of the world. Even the greatest deeds have
a hidden dark side, and the seeds of horror spring
up with others in the dreams of every budding life.

So from the beginning Cain grew up with the suggestion that first rights in everything were his due.
The will to power and the egotistical self-assertion
which were in his blood and ours too—for we are all
the children of Cain!—appear to him to be perfectly
legitimate. For him Abel is by no means his neighbor, who has his own rights in life. For him Abel is
neither a partner nor even a brother, but simply
exists to be used: "I, Cain, am the star, the privileged
one; but Abel is simply an extra on the stage. Abel
is of interest to me only in so far and as long as he
serves my career, as long as I can make a profit out

---

ing question: "Did Eve do right, etc." Every
mother in the audience is forced to face the
question of favoritism to her children.

Much of the feeling of the contemporary class
struggle, the "will to power and the egotistical
self-assertion which were in his blood and *ours
too* . . . appear to him (Cain) to be perfectly
legitimate." In this way Thielicke continues to
describe the present scene through *describing*
and *explaining* the *Bible* story. He strikes out
at the misuse of men by men, in *prophetic
fashion,* when he says "Abel is of interest to me

of him. Apart from this—that is, as a 'man'—he is nonexistent, he is a 'negligible quantity.' "

The figure of Cain really speaks volumes. It is actually a symbol. It blabs out all the callousness, contempt, and cynicism toward our neighbor that lies hidden in *my* heart too. For I too have within me the Cainitic urge to make myself the center and appraise all others only by whether they are useful or harmful to me. I am a small-scale Machiavelli, for whom all men are classified as either friends or enemies and the face of my neighbor threatens more and more to disappear.

Of course, at first all these feelings take place in secret. Apparently Cain himself did not realize what was happening inside of him. It took time until these secret tongues of fire in his heart burst into open flame.

---

only in so far . . . as I can make a profit out of him.

"The figure of Cain speaks volumes." Thielicke encourages the listener to *extend his imagination*. It is really a symbol. Thielicke *identifies* himself and all his listeners with Cain.

"I too have within me the Cainitic urge. . . ." "I am a small-scale Machiavelli."

Now comes the implied question: "How did it happen?" Here we have more of the prophetic element in Thielicke's message. "Cain did not realize. . . ." "He was a man who attended to his cultic duties." Thielicke puts into the same classification the "pharisees," "renaissance

At first the two still went together to their altars. Even Cain was not a godless man; he was a man who attended to his cultic duties. But what does that count for? Were not the scribes and Pharisees in the temple too? Did not the Renaissance popes celebrate mass? May it not be that many a regular churchgoer, who says "Forgive us our debts, as we forgive our debtors" when he utters the Lord's Prayer, really does not want his sins forgiven, because he has no desire whatsoever to recognize his sins? May it not be that he is by no means prepared to forgive the person who has injured or cheated him, that on the contrary he is actually pouring more oil on the flames of his hatred and thus even desires this fire in his heart and in a perverse way enjoys it? There is such a thing as getting a sensual pleasure from hate!

So what does it mean, after all, that Cain should come to the altar! Our wicked heart is quite capable

---

popes," and "many a regular churchgoer, who says 'forgive us our debts as we forgive'. . . but really does not want his sins forgiven." As a true *prophet,* Thielicke continues in this vein to persuade listeners who live in an unforgiven and unforgiving state to identify with Cain, but to realize what is happening to themselves. So he preaches a *theology* of forgiveness and of forgiving.

There is no break in the *continuity* of this sermon. It follows the natural outline of the story. The *narrative* is important but is second to the *identification* of the listener with the actors in the story and the *contemporizing* of its

of devising mischief even in holy places, and as we sing hymns the wolves may be howling in the cellars of our souls. While Cain is making his sacrifice he may perhaps have been far away from God.

He considers it quite natural that God should recognize him, that he should confirm him in his role as the strong one. He thinks, perhaps, that it must be so that God is on the side of the heaviest artillery, the biggest cars, and social superiority. And likewise it is no problem to him that God's scale of values should also assign this Abel to the category of an "also ran."

For just as Cain expects that Abel will dance to his tune, so he also expects the same of God. God is supposed to dance when Cain pipes. For somehow God has become for Cain a kind of celestial functionary who must execute exactly what Cain desires and what is right according to his standard of values, and thus according to what will make him feel confirmed in his own position.

And in this too Cain is an example par excellence of all men. When God takes the liberty to do something which we do not understand and which goes against the grain, we are immediately ready with

---

meaning. "As we sing hymns the wolves may be howling in the cellars of our souls." Cain is among those who think that God "should confirm him in his role as the stronger one . . . is on the side of the heaviest artillery, the biggest cars, and social superiority." The mood of this passage is very close to that of the prophet Amos. We can almost hear Thielicke add "and the white race."

the question—and we have already met with it in many variations—"How can God permit such a thing."

Job, for example, considered that it was right for the good to prosper and the wicked not to prosper. As long as God conformed to this favorite idea of his, to his conception of a moral world order, he was all right. But the first time God did something that did *not* fit into this system of co-ordinates, when his children died, his house burned down, and his flocks were destroyed, he went on strike and withdrew into the sulking corner of the religiously disappointed.

When the pastor in Ernst Wiechert's novel, *The Jeromin Children,* comes to the point where he no longer understands the catastrophe of war and the excesses of inhumanity and is unable to reconcile all this with his conception of a just God, he shakes his fist at the crucifix. Instead of the hand of God

---

How could God be angry with Cain's offering? Cain is among those who ask "How can God permit such a thing?" Here Thielicke cites the example of Job. He seems to assume considerable knowledge of the story on the part of his hearers. He *describes* what happened when God did something that did not fit into Job's "system of coordinates." "He went on strike. . . ."

The biblical *illustration* is followed by one from the novel by Ernst Wiechert. The pastor in Wiechert's story has the problem of many a modern man who faces "the catastrophe of war and the excesses of humanity and is unable to reconcile all this with his conception of a just

which supposedly holds the reins of the world, he sees only the hands of specters, and he says to a young person, "He *is* not, he *was* not, he never *will* be. Not the way it is written."

When God's thoughts are *actually* higher than our thoughts, we regard him as being refuted. For under all circumstances we want our thoughts to be the program according to which God operates. But the fact is that God is constantly *refuting* our human, all-too-human image of him. We, however, consider him refuted.

So Cain stands before the altar of God with a godless heart. God isn't acting in accord with his program—any more than He acted according to Job's program. He reacts differently from what Cain expects and considers right.

According to Cain's expectations, the smoke of his offering must rise to heaven like a sublime mushroom cloud. This was, in fact, an ancient sign

---

God, . . . and says, as he shakes his fist at the crucifix, . . . 'He *is* not, he *was* not, he never *will* be.' " In a situation such as this, Thielicke most certainly becomes *dramatic* in his *manner of delivery*; in this case he more than likely lifted his clenched fist to identify with the pastor in his *illustration*.

He uses the pronoun *we* and *our*, as he so often does, in the next paragraph as he seeks to make his thought *relevant* to his listeners. Throughout the sermon there has been a *confrontation* with the *need* for re-evaluation of relationships, which in itself is a *confrontation with decision*.

that God gratefully accepted a devout sacrifice. But in Abel's case, thinks Cain, considering his inferior station, there will be only a thin, fleeting bobtail of smoke which will go creeping and cowering along the ground. But it is just the opposite. The smoke of Abel's sacrifice rises up to heaven and Cain's offering is not accepted.

Thus God turns Cain's scale of values upside down. Consequently God is someone whom one must hate, for he permits himself to cancel out our calculation. Or consequently God is someone who doesn't exist at all. For, after all, what kind of an alibi does God have to offer? How can anybody exist who contradicts everything that I think makes sense? "He is not, he was not, he never will be. Not the way it is written," said the pastor in *The Jeromin Children* when he no longer could make sense of God.

Again, the story provides the *continuity* as Thielicke turns to the "smoke" of the sacrifices. Cain expects the smoke of his offering "to rise to heaven like a *sublime mushroom cloud*." The opposite, "a *thin, fleeting bobtail of smoke which will go creeping. . . .*" Thus he describes Cain's expectations. The opposite happens—*contrast*—the *description* is superb. "God turns Cain's scale of values upside down." Thielicke's *descriptions* and *explanations* are filled with *contrasts* and *comparisons*.

In the midst of his explication of the Bible story Thielicke again refers to *The Jeromin Children*. Thielicke seldom engages in the *repetition* of an *illustration* from literature in this way. He must have felt this one to be particu-

"So Cain was very angry, and his countenance fell." Now we know who it was against whom he was protesting with distorted countenance. It is none other than God, for God cut straight across everything that Cain thought was right. God failed to give him the self-confirmation he desired.

Up to this point all this, if I may express it in pointed terms, is still confined to the "religious sphere." These are still only the first stages of a story of rebellion. But in the very next moment this hidden drama between Cain and God spills over into the realm of external realities and human relationships. Renunciation of God brings with it renunciation of the brother. The form this hatred takes is envy. Cain is cankered and corroded with jealousy.

---

larly appropriate in describing the condition of his listeners or the people among whom they live. There is much *restatement* in this sermon, but very little actual *repetition*.

The *explanation* of what happens next is theological. It almost seems that Thielicke here is making too sharp a distinction between the "religious sphere" and the realm of "external realities and human relationships." This is actually contrary to the general handling of the religious and secular throughout the sermon. His application, however, is consistent with the rest of the sermon. "Renunciation of God brings with it renunciation of the brother." Thielicke continues to relate hatred for God with jealousy and envy, and considers what envy has to do with godlessness.

We must consider for a moment what envy has to do with Godlessness.

We moderns tend to psychologize everything and thus render it harmless. For us envy is something like a complex, like any other kind of inferiority feeling, which may possibly go back to a traumatic experience in our youth. In reality, however, much more than that happens when we are jealous. And since jealousy is an elemental process within us, since it can be a shattering, tormenting, destructive thing, we must take a good look at it.

When I am jealous I no longer see the other person as a "human being," as someone whom God has put in my way just as he is and furnished with particular gifts and accomplishments. I see only something about him, and most often something external. Perhaps I see in the other person only the owner of a car, while I go on pedaling a bicycle. Perhaps he may only have a bigger car than I, or his child has a doll that can open its eyes and say "Mama" whereas mine plays with a cheap thing from the five-and-dime—and is very happy with it! Or my neighbor has a better brand of vacuum cleaner, or my fellow

---

He is constantly exposing and exploding what he calls psychologizing. As for envy, we cannot psychologize it away.

He analyzes jealousy. Actually he describes how "I" see persons when I am jealous of them. He often uses the personal pronoun "I" when he wants to *confront* people with themselves and their own faults. At the same time he *identifies* with the listener in this way. His *illustrations* of jealousy in this lengthy paragraph come

worker has a workbench closer to the window. Or an assemblyman counts the number of lines reported in the press after every speech and is irked if his opponent is able to garner an average of a dozen words more than he does. Or a movie queen looks to see whether her pictures in the magazine are a quarter of a centimeter smaller than those of her rival. Or Cain watches to see whether Abel manages to make a higher annual profit with his flock than he—Cain—does with his cultivation of the soil.

It is incredible what trifles will kindle jealousy and how terribly I degrade the person of whom I am jealous, insofar as I look upon him only as the bearer of such trifles. I can literally grind myself to pieces with these petty, superficial differences in prestige. And all it does is rob me of my night's sleep. And meanwhile I no longer see the other person at all. All that he is to me—and how terrible this is!—is a representative of some petty, insignificant advantages.

I once realized the extent to which our neighbor actually disappears as a real person when someone who was jealous came to me and said, "Look, I always have bad luck, though I exert myself far more

from every level of society, from many areas of activity. It is almost as if he were attempting to include a probable area of jealousy for every person in the audience. At the end of the list he is careful to tie in the list with Cain and Abel.

In this part of the sermon Thielicke expounds on the undesirability, the awfulness of jealousy, on its "terrible" results. His use of the fear-anxiety side of the *expectation* factor which we

than Mr. Jones does and I have just as good a head as he does. But Jones always draws the winning ticket. His kids are always getting prizes in school while I have to spend good money to send my brats to an out-of-town school. And I'm always having bad luck with my personnel. But Jones has workers who are as good as gold. After all, anybody could get somewhere with people like that; that's no trick at all." And so the tale of woe went on.

Finally, with all this everlasting drawing of comparisons, "his countenance fell," just as Cain's did.

I then said to him, "So you would like to exchange for a lot of things that Jones has?"

"You can say that again," he said.

"But look here, my fellow," I went on, "whenever such exchanges are made you have to take the whole thing. So I ask you, would you want to trade with Mr. Jones in every respect, really everything? His marriage, his health, his age—he has already had his first heart trouble!—his temperament, his convictions, his faith?"

He looked at me somewhat taken aback and then said, "Perhaps I wouldn't trade with him in *every* respect, because I don't know him well enough; I

---

have called the *love-fear* (*motivation*) *factor* is obvious here. He uses one of his longest *illustrations* of this particular sermon at this point. It might be called "The Jealous Neighbor," though Thielicke merely says "our neighbor."

Thielicke becomes very *practical* after telling about the jealous neighbor, when he asks "but would you trade with him in every re-

wouldn't know *what* all I'd be getting out of the deal that I'd be stuck with."

"Look here," I said in closing the interview, "you are devoured by jealousy, but you are only envious of something *about* Mr. Jones. And you have only been seeing something *about* him. As far as you are concerned, he himself is unknown; you don't know him at all. Who this Mr. Jones is—with his secret cares and wounds, all things he has to struggle with, the things that get him down and nobody else knows about—what he really is, what he is in *secret*, and what he is as only God knows him, this you don't know and ultimately you're not *interested* in it all. Have you ever prayed for Mr. Jones? Only if you have brought yourself to do this in love, will you ever have any idea that in the eyes of God Mr. Jones is altogether different from what you choose to see in him when you enviously look at the outside of him."

---

spect?" In his "conversation with Mr. Jones," Thielicke raises a series of practical issues designed to *help* listeners in their relationships with their neighbors, particularly in relation to the problem of envy. These issues—in the nature of *practical help for living*—are approached through questions: "Do you know Mr. Jones? Have you ever prayed for Mr. Jones?"

"Only if you have . . . will you ever have any idea that in the eyes of God Mr. Jones is different. . . ." Again the *theological explanation*; Thielicke has tied together the man-God-neighbor relationship. Here is a most perceptive

And this is actually the way it is. Only he who has some conception of the fact that we are children who have a Father—a Father who alone really knows us —and that we are in need of forgiveness and help, that we are bleeding from secret wounds and have black stretches in our life that nobody knows about, but which Jesus knows, only he can accept another person from the hand of God and let him be what he is—even when it's hard for him and envy leaps up within him.

But because this is so, it will be quite futile for me to combat jealousy merely by will power and auto-suggestion and by trying to doctor the accounts between the other person and myself and get more favorable results for myself by these everlasting comparisons. No, envy can be combatted only by letting God give me a new faith, a faith that accepts the other person just as he has been sent to me by a higher hand, as someone who has his place and function in God's plan exactly as I have, as some-

---

summation of our needs—"a Father . . . forgiveness and help, . . . bleeding from secret wounds . . . black stretches . . . nobody knows about, but which Jesus knows; only he [who has a Father] can accept another person from the hand of God and let him be what he is, . . ."

In the paragraph from which we have just quoted and in the next we have the highest form of *practical help for living* that a preacher may help to provide for his listeners.

How can envy be combatted? In Thielicke's answer there is an unavoidable *confrontation with decision* for every man in the necessity to

one who confronts me with the command of love
and in whom God's higher thoughts come to meet
me.

But how can I do all this and carry it out if I have
fallen out with Him who sent him and made him
what he is?

Now I should feel that I had been thoroughly mis-
understood if what I have said, namely, that I must
accept the other person from God's hand, were taken
merely as pious rhetoric or cheap pastoral consola-
tion. I am utterly serious about this and I believe
that here we are dealing with a fundamental reality
of life. The corruption of our relationship to our
neighbor and our own self-destruction—that self-
tormenting feud that jealousy stirs up within us—

---

accept the brother. Furthermore, "envy can be
combatted only by letting God give me a new
faith, a faith that accepts the other person just
as . . . as someone who confronts me with the
command of love and in whom God's higher
thoughts come to me." Thielicke's hearers often
said that his religion is *love to the neighbor.*
Here faith with love is proclaimed as the answer to the problem of envy; it is also used as
a *motivating force* in this part of the sermon.

Then follows a key question: "But how can
I do all this and carry it out if I have fallen out
with Him who sent him [the neighbor] and
made him what he is?"

At this point Thielicke enters into his dis-
course in a most *personal* way. It is the only
time in the sermon that he uses the personal

can *actually* be overcome only by faith. We must learn to accept the other person from God's hand.

That is all there is to it, but it is really the whole cure. But, after all, we can accept something from this hand only if we trust it, even when it does that which is different from what we wished or thought right. The point is that Cain did not accept Abel. This and nothing else was the root of the whole calamity. For Cain, the elder brother, Abel was the great disruption of his concept of life. So Cain withdrew his trust from God when God, quite contrary to Cain's ideas, accepted his brother and left him,

---

pronoun with the full intent of staking his personal feelings, his whole *personality* so directly behind the "I". "I am utterly serious about this and I believe that we are dealing with a fundamental reality in life."

What is the fundamental reality in life that confronts us? "I must accept the other person from God's hand." This demands trust, for "we can accept something from this [God's] hand only if we trust it."

Thus, says Thielicke, "The corruption of our relationship to our neighbor . . . can. *actually* be overcome only by faith."

Thielicke turns again to the biblical account; this determines his *continuity*. Cain did not accept Abel. We ask, is this a theology basic to human relationship? Thielicke says that Cain withdrew his trust from God when God, contrary to Cain's ideas, accepted his brother.

Cain, for a moment in the dark. And because he fell out with God, he also fell out with his brother.

All this, as we have said, is at first only an episode in a man's intimate relationship to God in his heart. But down in this inner domain, this so-called "religious sphere," is located the switchboard from which all the switches of our life are operated.

At first the story moves only in the realm of externals such as that his countenance fell and began

---

When Cain fell out with God, he also fell out with his brother.

Thielicke seems to want it both ways: because Cain did not accept Abel he lost his trust in God; because he fell out with his God, he also fell out with his brother. Was it both? If so, might it not have been better to have made it more explicit? We ask the question: Is communion between God and man ultimately based on a triangular relationship, a man-man-God relationship? Thielicke seems to imply that this is so, but he does not make it explicit. Thielicke speaks about "intimate relationship to God [He believes in an intimate relationship with God.]," and about a so-called "religious sphere," where the switchboard is located from which "all switches of our life are operated." The *illustration* conveys the point that all that was wrong in the center of Cain's life was operative, at first, at the "switchboard" center and only became external as the result of continued hostility.

to reflect hostility. They follow the furtive glances
at his brother and that clairvoyant jealousy that
immediately notices whenever Abel has some bit
of advantage. The hatred condenses into complexes,
and the image of the brother disappears behind
caricatures and specters which poisoned imagination make of him. Then—and here is a new phase!—
God intervenes with a warning, puts himself in his
way, and tells him that sin is lying in wait at his
door and desiring to get at him. But how can Cain
ever hear this warning when he has long since
shaken off the Warner? Then follows his invitation
to Abel: "Come, let us go out to the field to have a
talk with each other."

Only now does what began as a protest against
God and what at first was only a thought beneath
the surface in the interior of the self become an act.
The deadly ax swished down upon Abel.

Thielicke's *explanation* of the development
of the hostility is exceedingly *thought provoking*. "Hatred condenses into complexes, and the
image of the brother disappears behind caricatures and specters which poisoned imagination
make of him."

Thielicke returns to the *continuity* of the
story. "God intervenes with a warning," which
Cain cannot hear because he "has long since
shaken off the Warner." Then follows his invitation to Abel: "Come, let us. . . ."

The protest against God ends in murder. Here
Thielicke shows a deep *psychological understanding* of the nature of protest when he says

But this is not the end of it. Cain's solo hatred soon becomes a whole chorus of hate and Cain's murder is followed by war and rumors of war and every brutal and subtle form of murder that history has developed. That *one* perilous spark that flared up in Cain's heart soon outshone the sacrificial fires on a thousand altars, became a prairie fire of blood vengeance and battlefields, and one day, as Robert Jungk says, will become brighter and more consuming than a "thousand suns" and lay the earth in ashes.

---

that "what at first was only a thought beneath the surface in the interior of the self became an act." It could as well be called a *theological insight*—an understanding of the nature of sin?

Again, he relates the story to history, as at the beginning of the sermon: "Cain's murder is followed by war and rumors of war and every brutal and subtle form of murder." His *credibility* at this point is certainly not questioned by a modern German listener. A vivid *description* of the "spark that flared up in Cain's heart and soon outshone the sacrificial fires on a thousand altars . . ." is followed by the mention of Robert Jungk's prophecy. This *quotation* of Jungk's prophecy of apocalyptic proportions seems somewhat extreme, but it undoubtedly causes the listener to think about man's ultimate destructive capability. By his hearers Thielicke is usually not considered a *prophet of doom.*

Why do we talk so much about atomic fires and why do we surrender to the self-destroying "lust for downfall?" Why do we indulge in visions of dread? Why have the novels about the future—we have referred to this before—long since ceased to wax enthusiastic over the progress of mankind toward undreamed-of heights of happiness? Why is it that today they present only delineations of terror?

The story of Cain and Abel calls us to order, because it says to us: "Don't keep looking spellbound into the atomic holocaust of the cosmos that threatens your earth, but look at the little sparks from which they come; look at the Cain within you. Return again to the altar and present your sacrifice in a way different from the way Cain did. All honor to your diplomatic endeavors and your peace organizations, but all this is only symptom therapy; it never gets beyond external patchwork if you refuse to go to the innermost seat of the disease, if you do not lay yourselves upon this sacrificial altar in order that God may be able to make something new of you.

Even more *thought provoking* is his next paragraph, in which he asks why we engage in so much talk of atomic fires. "Why do we indulge in visions of dread?" Why do novelists today "present only delineations of terror?" He turns to a *helpful, constructive* note, perhaps to an *inspirational* thought. "Look at the little sparks from which they came, . . . look at the Cain within you." This is a part of his attempt to *confront* the listener *with a challenge,* an *appeal*. More directly he *appeals* to the listener to "return again to the altar and present your sacrifice. . . ."

"Why do you gaze so spellbound at rockets and future flights into space?" this story asks us. "Are you trying to divert attention from yourselves, you who are still bleeding from the wound of Cain? I am an ancient story from primitive times, but it's your story, and the question it puts to you reaches farther than the cosmic dimensions which you are now working to open up.

"You are always thinking about the remotest goals," says this ballad of Cain and Abel, "but you forget that everything depends upon the starting point. You stand at the altar and call yourselves Christians, you keep burning incense to "Christian civilization." Do you have any idea of what this means? Have you forgotten that all this is a matter of facing God, and nobody else but God—and not the scarecrow of a windy, shallow Christianity or an even more windy, conventional church?

He then speaks as if the story itself is speaking to the listeners: "I am an ancient story from primitive times." But he does not maintain this personification as he continues, "but it's your story." The ballad speaks again: "You are always thinking of the remotest goals, but you forget. . . ." Thielicke is almost scathing here in his *prophetic* mood. "You keep burning incense to 'Christian civilization'. Do you have any idea what this means?" His style here becomes somewhat dramatic—he is not often so "hard," so critical. These are burning words: "scarecrow of a windy, shallow Christianity or even more windy conventional church. 'For God's sake' says this story, 'it's a matter of God, of your being at peace with him.'"

"For God's sake," says this story, "it's a matter of God, of your being at peace with him. Everything else is charlatanry, religious or humanistic humbug, as long as this *one* thing is not in order. Your humanity becomes humanitarian drool and drivel, if you do not accept the existence of Abel, if you do not accept your neighbor from the high and holy hand of God, and if you no longer see his face gazing at you from the face of your competitors or even that of a functionary."

It is a constant source of amazement to me—you will permit me to add this in conclusion—that Jesus Christ never set forth a reform program for the abolition of slavery, for a new system of law and society, and a new and better world order—which, after all is done by every revival movement that has

---

His challenge comes again—here is *confrontation* with the stark facts of human nature and of the human predicament.

Thielicke *compares* the acceptance of the existence of Abel from the hand of God with other religious or humanistic solutions in somewhat drastic words such as "everything else is charlatanry. . . ." Here again we have the *repetition* of his main emphasis, framed in the language of *contrast*. His language is highly *descriptive*.

He launches into a recital of all that Jesus Christ did not do: "He never set forth a reform program, etc." We have heard this before, but when Thielicke says it, we look for something to follow it in a positive vein. He proceeds to summarize the basic biblical and theological support for all that he has been saying. "All that

any respect for itself at all. All that Jesus said was that we have a Father who is seeking us, a Father who grieves over the last thief and the last hangman beneath the cross, and plants a spark of true love in the corrupt heart of the woman who was a sinner. And then he lets us see our neighbor anew *beneath* the eyes and *with* the eyes of this our Father.

We must get this straight. He does not give us a new view of society or of so-called humanity—what is that anyway?—but rather makes us *see anew* the blind man there at the corner, the prostitute in her self-despising, the rich young ruler with his inner emptiness, the old woman in her loneliness.

Jesus said was that we have a Father who is seeking us, a Father who grieves . . . etc." He is describing God as known through Jesus Christ in the gospels. His final key sentence is "And then he [Jesus] lets us see our neighbor anew beneath the eyes and with the eyes of this our Father."

He uses a rhetorical device: "We understand," or "do we understand?" (*Verstehen wir:*) The expression is not as insistent as Doberstein's "We must get this straight." What is it that we should understand? It is that Jesus does not give us a new view of *society (Gesellschaft)* or of so-called humanity (*Menschheit*)—what is that anyway? New societal or humanistic schemes do not deal with the problem of the Cain in us. For Thielicke what Christ does for us is to make us "See anew the blind man there at the corner, the prostitute in her self-despising, the rich young ruler. . . ." This is basic for Thielicke in Christian *theology*.

He always shows us only the human being next to us. He makes us responsible only for a single milligram of the world's great burden. And even he himself, this Jesus Christ, whose arms embrace the globe and to whom has been committed all power in heaven and earth, he too has time to be present for the *one* individual who needs him today, even though this one individual be only a poor wretch and certainly no key figure for the Christianization of the earth. For this one individual is a greeting and a charge from his Father.

When I hear this message of my neighbor and follow it in obedience, then at *one* small place I shall

---

Throughout this part of the sermon he seeks to take his congregation along with him by using the words "we" and "us." He does this in the *restatement* of his central themes, when he says, "He always shows *us* only the human being next to *us*." Here again there is *confrontation with decision:* "He makes *us* responsible only for a single milligram of the world's great burden." We may well ask the question: Is this not an oversimplification of the Christian's task? But Thielicke resumes: ". . . even he, himself, this Jesus, . . . has time to be present for the *one* individual who needs him today, even though . . . poor wretch and certainly no key figure for the Christianization of the earth. For this one individual is a greeting and a charge from his Father."

Thielicke does several things in the above paragraphs: he brings confidence and comfort to lonely individuals in his congregation; he

traverse the misery and discord of the world. Christians are not reformers, but they walk through life with their fellow men. The meek and the loving will inherit the earth, because they walk through it and suffer with it. But the conquerors are condemned to ruin. For, as Reinhold Schneider said, "The doers will never take heaven by force."

---

continues to support the *central point* of his sermon; and he makes a point of discounting the efforts of some who are concerned with various schemes for human betterment not based on Jesus' way of dealing with the needs of individuals.

Not every one is satisfied with Thielicke's insistence that "Christians are not reformers." However, with his insistence that "they walk through life with their fellow men," few among his listeners or readers will quarrel. Many of them will have been inspired to make a new attempt to "walk with the neighbor."

In the second from last paragraph of the sermon Thielicke speaks of the "meek," the "loving," who will "inherit the earth, because they walk through it and suffer with it." Again he introduces one of the great *biblical contrasts:* "But the conquerors are condemned to ruin."

Once more he quotes an *authority,* Reinhold Schneider, who said, "The doers will never take heaven by force." Although there is no devil, as such, in this sermon, as there is in so many of Thielicke's sermons, still one almost begins to think there is an adversary. Who *is* this oppo-

Jesus Christ would redeem the Cain within us and
only so does he redeem the world. Love conquers
all, because it traverses the world's misery at a
single point, at the point where my neighbor stands
—that neighbor whom I find so hard to love and who

---

nent? Or, perhaps we should ask, who *are they?*
Could they be those who ignore the central
point of this sermon—that God redeems individuals through the love of a man for his neighbor.
For Thielicke, any other gospel "misses the
point."

Is he against "doing good works," against all
"social gospel?" It is interesting to note that
the same man who remembers Reinhold Schneider's saying, as quoted above, in the same meeting more than likely sponsored the collection
of a large offering for some worthy cause in
East Germany and often raises his voice for or
against current issues in university, city, or
nation. Moreover, his congregation is quite
aware of all this.

Nevertheless, for Thielicke, being a disciple
of Christ is a matter of the spirit, a matter involving personal change, a matter of relationships; it is a matter of relationship, both to
God and to man. And "man" means the neighbor
"whom God put right where he is."

We come now to the final sentences of the
sermon. As Thielicke has so often emphasized
in his writings and in his interviews with representatives of the press, the closing words
of each sermon must contain something for

perhaps also makes things hard for me. But God
himself put him right where he is. I can overlook
him and I can hurry past him, but then I shall run
straight into the arms of God. And if I do that, what
[who] will God be for me? What will I answer him
when he says, "Where is Abel your brother?"

---

every man and every woman in the congregation. So we look at his closing words in this
message to see what it is that he wants to leave
with his congregation in his conclusion.

The first sentence is a summary of the central
point of the message as related to Jesus Christ.
"Jesus Christ would [wants to] redeem the
Cain within us and only so does he redeem the
world." Then there is the emphasis, the *repetition* of the emphasis, on love toward the neighbor. And the strong suggestion that if I hurry
past the neighbor I will run right into the arms
of God. Here he is very close to using a *fear*
type of motivation. This is felt again when he
asks, in his closing sentence, "What will I answer him when he [God] says, 'Where is Abel
your brother?'"

The last sentence had a secondary purpose.
The title of the follow-up sermon in the series
had already been announced earlier in the service, either in a printed circular or from the pulpit. The secondary purpose was again to remind the people that the next sermon title
would be "Where is Abel your brother?"

Thus, in the final paragraph of the sermon
Thielicke *met* the *requirements of preaching*

expressed in terms of *lay expectation factors* as related to the following characteristics: the *theology of the sermon; inspirational quality; love - fear, motivational quality; thought provoking quality;* a satisfactory *format, continuity;* and *confrontation with decision.* In addition, he ties in his message with the message to follow in the series.

Thus far in this study of "The Cain Within Us" we have related parts of the sermon to each of the *lay expectation factors* excepting *credibility, comprehensibility, preparation, preacher's personality,* and *range of subjects.*

The last, *range of subjects,* hardly comes in question in a single sermon, even though one might say that Thielicke touches on many topics in this sermon. Actually he adheres closely to the central themes of the text. His continuity is determined by the passage of scripture as related to the needs of the people.

Little can be learned about the *preacher's personality* from a printed sermon excepting by way of inferences from the character of the thought, the quality of the words and the order of the format. In this regard the sermon speaks for itself regarding the personality of the preacher.

With regard to *preparation* there is every evidence of careful attention to the requirements of preaching and to the development of the sermon in its completeness. His *style* as far as can be ascertained by his *choice of words, symbols, illustrations,* and by its *continuity* is evidently the result of much thoughtful and careful preparation.

Is the sermon *comprehensible?* The vocabulary, in German, is on about the same level as Doberstein's English translation. Here and there Doberstein uses a word in translation that seems to be more difficult to understand than its German counterpart in the original. The opposite may also be true in a few instances. There is probably nothing in the vocabulary as such that would not be readily understood by the average high school graduate. This is not to say that his meaning is always clear to all of his listeners. That would depend on the hearer's background, interests, and on his effort to comprehend.

The factor of *credibility* has been mentioned only once in the discussion of "The Cain Within Us." The over-all *feeling tone,* the *expressive speech* quality of the sermon can only be inferred from the words and the thought. To one who has heard Thielicke preach a number of times, this sounds like a very "serious," a very "intensive" sermon. The fact that the preacher never departs for very long from the *biblical text* would enhance his credibility with most of his hearers as judged by the almost universal interest in *biblical preaching* on the part of persons interviewed in this study. Thielicke's *theological-doctrinal* thought is continually supported by reference to the *biblical* material. The fact that he makes the biblical passage apply to the contemporary life of real people adds to his credibility. His quotations from outside the Bible are not as numerous in this sermon as in some of his sermons, but they are from well known and reliable sources. His first *extra-biblical quotation,* for example, is from Goethe, the favorite German poet.

The constant effort Thielicke makes in this sermon to relate the ancient "ballad" to the contemporary forms of speech and thought not only add *realism* and *relevance* to the sermon but make it more credible to many of his listeners. In other words, the twin-factors, *relevance* and *credibility,* are enhanced for many listeners, especially for members of the student generation, by his frank dealing with the story as a "ballad," as a symbol of beginnings, and especially as descriptive of "all times."

As was said at the beginning of the study of this sermon, beyond frankly speaking of the story as a "ballad," Thielicke does not raise critical questions about the text.

It is also worthy of note that he makes nothing at all of the traditional interpretation of the cause of Cain's unacceptable sacrifice; he does not even mention it. We refer to the traditional discussions of the relative merit of "blood sacrifice" as against any other. Rather, he finds the solution to the meaning of the "ballad" in the character of the brothers and in their relationships to each other and to God. Because of all these considerations we may assume that the element of credibility was most certainly strongly represented in this sermon.

Postscript: As a postscript to the analysis of Thielicke's sermon, "The Cain Within Us," we have added a study of the use of pronouns, names, and other references to persons including those to deity as used in the sermon. As indicated in Table 3 on the following page, perhaps the most significant insight gleaned from this exercise is the realization that Thielicke has a way of taking his congregation along with him in his development of the thought of the sermon that is best illustrated by the number of times he says "we" and "us." When he uses "we" he includes himself as a member of the vast congregation. According to our count he thus included himself with the congregation 88 times in the sermon. Having made the same count in numerous sermons by Thielicke, we know that this is about the average number of times he does this in his sermons.

His use of the personal pronoun "I" with reference to himself alone varies in his sermons from two to twenty times. In this particular sermon it was used 14 times, which is considerably above the mean for Thielicke. In this sermon he also used the pronoun "I" a great many times (30 times) in identifying himself with the members of the congregation and even with Cain. Usually this usage of "I" is found in much more limited fashion in his sermons. Six examples of this usage are found in the

Table 3

THE CAIN WITHIN US: A POSTSCRIPT

The following tabulation is a result of a study (lit. a counti
of Thielicke's use of pronouns and of his use of other forms
personal address, reference to deity, use of the names of
actors in the story, and reference to Holy Scriptures.

Number of times used	Form of address, with explanation (pronoun, name, etc.)	
14	I	Strictly personal, reference to self
30	I	Self, but including identification with the members of the congregation
12	I	Spoken for or in place of an actor in Bible story or illustration
2	I (me)	Personification of the Bible story
88	We, us	Referring to the members of the congregation and including the speaker
66	You, he	Any or all listeners
95	He, they	Actors or participants in the story and in the illustrations, etc.
3	They	"The Devout"
3	Who?	*Who,* when used in questions
13	They	The people, when the people are the actors
83	God	God, God's, God's hand, of God, including pronouns used for God
7	Jesus	Used of Jesus as pertaining to his earthly life, including pronouns
13	Jesus Christ	Lord, Savior, including pronouns referring to Christ
4	Father	Referring to God
2	Bible	Holy Scriptures
58	Cain	Cain as personal, Cain as portraying evil in human life
30	Abel	· Abel as personal, Abel as representing the neighbor
0	Satan	Satan, devil, demonic, evil powers, adversary

Source: Lay Expectation Factor Study, 1968, M. Dirks, B. U. S. T.

concluding paragraph of the sermon. Speaking of the "neighbor," he says, " 'I' can overlook him and 'I' can hurry past him, but then 'I' shall run straight into the arms of God." In sentences such as this one, Thielicke obviously means to include everyone who will consent to identify himself with the sense of the sentence. Also, note that he uses "I" numerous times in the place of the actors in the story and in the recounting of the experiences of persons in his illustrations.

The importance of the biblical account to the development of the sermon is supported by the number of times the name of "God" and the names of "Cain" and "Abel" are used.

One final item of interest in Table 3 is the fact that there is no devil, no Satan in the entire sermon. Apparently here the figure of Cain takes the place of the chief adversary found in many of Thielicke's sermons. In a similar manner Abel represents the neighbor.

In concluding our sermon analysis we submit that the sermon, "The Cain Within Us," may be looked upon as an exhibit to demonstrate that the elements of preaching as assessed by laymen and represented by the twenty lay expectation factors would be shown to be positively dealt with as found in the preaching of Thielicke.

Chapter 7

THE PEOPLE RESPOND—WHAT THE CONGREGATION SEES AND HEARS

*Characteristics of Preaching Mentioned by
Laymen As Basic to Their Response
to Preaching*

Thus far we have introduced our purpose in the study of *Lay Expectation Factors,* our reasons for selecting Helmut Thielicke, in particular, and also Woldemar Lein as ministers worthy of study in this connection, and we have described briefly the procedures used in the course of our study. This was followed with an introduction to the churches and the people interviewed—the people whose responses we are to share with the reader in this chapter.

We have given special attention to the growth and development of Helmut Thielicke as a man, as a preacher, and as a writer. We have discussed his ideals and principles in preaching and how these relate to the lay expectation factors emphasized by laymen. We have analyzed one of his sermons in order to illustrate how intimately the L E Fs are bound up in the production of an effective sermon.

All this has in a sense been introductory to the main purpose of this book which is to report what the layman expects from preaching and how laymen have responded to the preaching of Helmut Thielicke and Woldemar Lein in terms of twenty lay expectation factors.

In the study our first step was to achieve the arranging of the *Ideal Lay Expectation Factors* into a relatively stable rank order by use of the Q-sort method. Tabulation of the early results on L L tests of the Ideal Q-sort indicated that a relatively stable hierarchy of the 20 L E Fs would be achieved without extending the testing beyond the number of subjects chosen in the random sample of Christuskirche members. This was confirmed when a Spearman rho comparison of rank order between the first 30 subjects interviewed and the total number of 55 L Ls indicated a correlation of .99 plus. In no case was the rank order changed by more than one place by the addition of the last 25 subjects.[1]

On the Thielicke Listener Ideal Q-sort, administered to 82 persons, comparison of the first half with the total rank order of 82 subjects yielded a Spearman rho of .99 plus, and comparison of the second half with the total yields a .98 correlation. Since the student group of interviewees had been most at variance with the total sample of 82 T Ls in several respects, a Spearman rank order comparison was made between the 18 students and the 82 T Ls. Even this resulted in a rank order coefficient of .98 plus. Only the group of 8 ministers proved to be slightly more variant from the total group on the Ideal Q-sort with a Spearman rho of .85.

The relative stability of the Ideal Q-sort ratings is further illustrated by Table 4, page 254, which lists the results of the T and L Q-sorts in parallel columns together with the mean Q-sort value rating on each ideal lay expectation factor.

The reader may know that the "choices" on the Q-sort were weighted as follows:

Most important ... 4
Very important.... 3
Important 2
Less important 1

The mean Q-sort value rating on each factor was computed by the simple process of multiplying the number of choices in each position by the number indicated above and adding the number of choices as thus weighted and dividing by the number of subjects interviewed.

The Spearman rank order computation on the TL and LL Ideal L E F comparison as set side by side in Table 4 yielded a .91 correlation. This is considered highly significant when some of the basic differences between the two groups are considered.

Table 5, Page 255 is the result of combining the TL and LL Ideal L E F ranks by finding the means of each pair of factors and listing them in order. The Spearman rho correlations of .97 and .96 between the LL Ideal and TL Ideal rank orders, respectively, when compared with the combined Ideal rank order as listed in Table 5

Table 4

20 IDEAL LAY EXPECTATION FACTORS
Comparing Q-Sort Ratings by
82 Thielicke and 55 Lein Listeners

THIELICKE   LEIN

Mean Q-sort Rating

THIELICKE			LEIN
credibility	3.60	3.58	Bible
practical help	3.26	3.35	practical help
comprehensibility	3.16	3.22	credibility
theological content	3.12	3.02	decision
relevancy	3.08	3.00	theological content
Bible	3.01	3.00	thought provoking
decision	2.80	2.93	comprehensibility
thought provoking	2.80	2.86	relevancy
continuity	2.62	2.60	inspirational
attention holding	2.46	2.53	attention holding
delivery	2.32	2.36	continuity
illustrations	2.31	2.36	prophetic voice
inspirational	2.31	2.33	illustrations
personality	2.31	2.27	personality
prophetic voice	2.11	2.22	delivery
authority	1.92	1.87	authority
preparation	1.83	1.69	preparation
originality	1.78	1.67	love - fear
love - fear	1.74	1.60	originality
range of subjects	1.46	1.55	range of subjects

Source: Lay Expectation Factor Study, 1968, M. Dir
B. U. S. T.

Table 5

MEAN IDEAL LAY EXPECTATION FACTORS

For 82 Thielicke and 55 Lein Listeners

Lay Expectation factors	Mean Q-sort Rating
1. credibility	3.41
2. practical help for living	3.31
3. Bible, use of	3.29
4. theological content	3.06
5. comprehensibility	3.04
6. relevancy	2.97
7. decision, confrontation with	2.92
8. thought provoking	2.90
9. attention holding	2.50
10. continuity (organization)	2.49
11. inspirational quality	2.45
12. illustrations, use of	2.32
13. preacher's personality	2.29
14. delivery, manner of (style)	2.27
15. prophetic voice	2.23
16. authority, basis and use of	1.90
17. preparation, evidence of	1.76
18. love - fear (quality of motivation)	1.70
19. originality	1.69
20. range of subjects	1.50

Source: Lay Expectation Factor Study, 1968, M. Dirks, B.U.S.T.

gave indication of the practicality of using the rank order of the combined Ideal L E F list, compiled from the results of the total of 137 Q-sort tests, for purposes of comparison with the Q-sort results on the preaching of Thielicke and Lein, and also with the *scale value ratings* derived from the results of the G P C (General Preaching Characteristics) Test administered to the 137 T and L listeners.

In order to display them more graphically the Q-sort evaluations on the 20 Ideal L E Fs are presented in Graph I, on Page 257 under the title "Ideal Lay Expectation Factors of 137 Listeners of Thielicke and Lein with Mean Depicted." Graph I and Tables 4 and 5 provide visual portrayal of what the layman expects to hear in the sermon hour, or perhaps put more inclusively, of what he expects to experience in the preaching of the minister.

The results from the Ideal Q-sort testing indicate that although there are certain basic differences in expectation factor rankings, L and T listeners were generally agreed on what is (1) most important, (2) very important, (3) important, and (4) less important.

L Ls rate *use of the Bible, inspirational quality, prophetic voice,* and *confrontation with decision* generally higher than T Ls rate these factors. T Ls, on the other hand, rate *credibility, continuity, comprehensibility,* and *relevancy* higher than L Ls rate them. The reader may make his own more exact mathematical com-

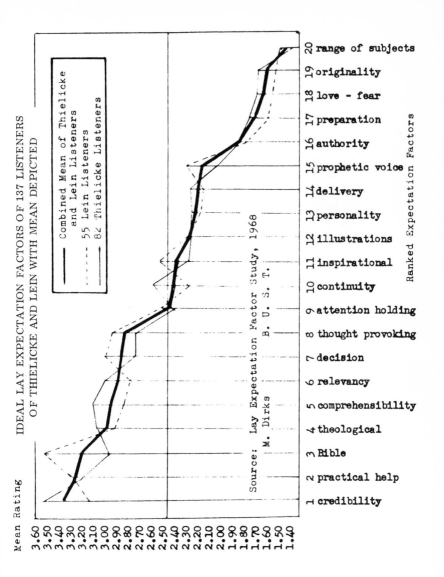

IDEAL LAY EXPECTATION FACTORS OF 137 LISTENERS
OF THIELICKE AND LEIN WITH MEAN DEPICTED

Mean Rating

—— Combined Mean of Thielicke
   and Lein Listeners
---- 55 Lein Listeners
—·— 82 Thielicke Listeners

Source: Lay Expectation Factor Study, 1968
         M. Dirks   B. U. S. T.

Ranked Expectation Factors

20 range of subjects
19 originality
18 love - fear
17 preparation
16 authority
15 prophetic voice
14 delivery
13 personality
12 illustrations
11 inspirational
10 continuity
9 attention holding
8 thought provoking
7 decision
6 relevancy
5 comprehensibility
4 theological
3 Bible
2 practical help
1 credibility

parisons by referring to Table 4. He may note that the widest divergence between the two groups was in use of the Bible at .57. On this factor students at 2.76 and ministers at 2.38 helped to pull down the T L rating. Perhaps the most unexpected result of the Ideal L E F testing was the very high place given credibility. Among the T L interviewees no particular subgroup was responsible for this high rating.

According to his own interest the reader may wish to take note of other significant differences between the choices of T and L listeners. By this time he may also wish to review the laymen's definition of our terms, for the meaning of the lay expectation factors. To do this he may wish to turn back to pages 28 to 30, for we are now ready to see how the laymen have evaluated the preaching of Thielicke and Lein in the second use of the Q-sort.

How Laymen Responded to the Preaching of Thielicke and Lein

Where the Ideal Q-sort revealed the layman's ideal expectations in regard to preaching, the Q-sort on the actual preaching of the ministers gave us a descriptive view of what the laymen considered most important in a positive sense in the preaching. Characteristics or factors of the preaching involving negative aspects were placed lower in the Q-sort rating than those with predominantly positive qualities.

So now, how did 137 persons, in terms of the 20 L E Fs, describe the preaching of two men, both of them known as superior preachers in the areas of their active ministry? On Page 260, in Table 6, the mean rating on each factor in the preaching of Thielicke and Lein may be studied separately and in comparison with the total picture of each preacher, or in comparison with the picture of the other preacher.

And in Graph II, Page 261, the 20 characteristics as rated by the respective listeners to the preaching of Thielicke and Lein are plotted alongside of the line established by the combined groups on the Ideal L E Fs as listed in Table 5. As this graph demonstrates both lines in a general sense follow the *ideal* line of the ranked L E Fs. However, the peculiar and characteristic qualities in the preaching of each man are clearly portrayed.

It is interesting to note that the Lein line runs somewhat more nearly parallel to the line of the ranked Ideal L E Fs than does the Thielicke line. This difference is clearly seen statistically in the Spearman rho correlation of .87 on the L rank order comparison as against a .68 Spearman rho correlation on the Thielicke rank order comparison, when each is compared with the Ideal rank order.

What have the laymen actually said about the preaching of Thielicke and Lein? Before we attempt to answer this question we must reiterate that the Q-sort is a forced test. Moreover,

Table 6

20 LAY EXPECTATION FACTORS IN THE PREACHING OF THIELICKE AND LEIN
Comparing Q-sort Ratings by 82 T and 55 L Listeners

THIELICKE   LEIN

Mean Q-sort Rating

THIELICKE			LEIN
theological content	3.22	3.56	credibility
relevancy	3.12	3.40	Bible
comprehensibility	3.02	3.24	comprehensibility
personality	2.98	3.20	theological content
credibility	2.96	2.89	thought provoking
illustrations	2.80	2.87	continuity
Bible	2.71	2.87	practical help
attention holding	2.66	2.65	attention holding
continuity	2.61	2.56	decision
delivery	2.54	2.55	personality
practical help	2.50	2.49	relevancy
inspirational	2.48	2.38	delivery
originality	2.44	2.36	illustrations
thought provoking	2.41	2.29	range of subjects
decision	2.21	2.16	inspirational
prophetic voice	2.17	1.91	authority
preparation	1.98	1.76	preparation
range of subjects	1.84	1.71	love-fear
authority	1.84	1.65	prophetic voice
love-fear	1.51	1.47	originality

Source: Lay Expectation Factor Study, 1968, M. Di
B.U.S.T.

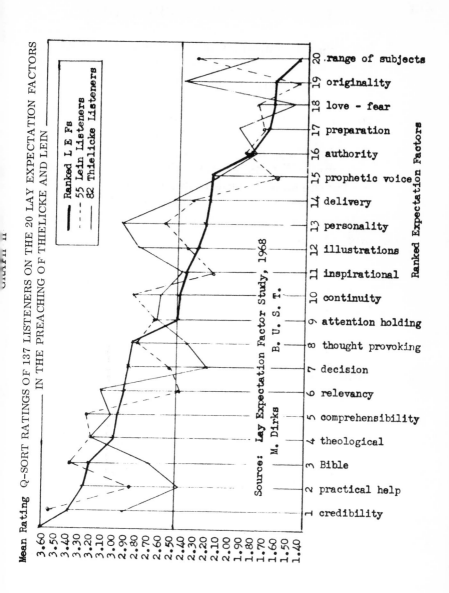

GRAPH II

Mean Rating Q-SORT RATINGS OF 137 LISTENERS ON THE 20 LAY EXPECTATION FACTORS
IN THE PREACHING OF THIELICKE AND LEIN

Ranked L E Fs
55 Lein Listeners
82 Thielicke Listeners

Source: Lay Expectation Factor Study, 1968
M. Dirks   B. U. S. T.

Ranked Expectation Factors

1 credibility
2 practical help
3 Bible
4 theological
5 comprehensibility
6 relevancy
7 decision
8 thought provoking
9 attention holding
10 continuity
11 inspirational
12 illustrations
13 personality
14 delivery
15 prophetic voice
16 authority
17 preparation
18 love - fear
19 originality
20 range of subjects

with the exception of ten persons who were interviewed as members of both sample groups,
the ratings were made by two distinctively different groups of listeners. Because of these
reasons it is not possible to make unqualified
assertions on the effectiveness of the two
preachers by simply comparing mean scores
arithmetically as a basis for our conclusions.
So for the sake of emphasis we repeat that *what
can be seen* from our results is: *which characteristics,* in the opinion of the respective listening sample, *most mark the peculiar ability of
the preacher* whose preaching is the focus of
attention.

Here again the Spearman formula for rank
correlation is a help in comparing the T and L
Preaching Q-sort results. It yields a significant
positive .66 correlation. This indicates that
there are significant similarities in the rank
order but it also shows that there are divergen-
cies in regard to which characteristics are considered the important and less important factors
in the preaching of the two men.

Certainly the widest divergence from the
layman's ideal expectation was registered by
T Ls on *originality*. Listeners generally feel
that Thielicke is usually original in his ideas
and approach to preaching, but not all agree
that originality can be a highly important characteristic of preaching. In the Lein Listeners
rating on originality there was a heavy mode
of 35 on less important. Apparently Lein's

preaching does not readily bring this characteristic to mind. A number of persons interviewed stated in one way or another that originality is not one of Pastor Lein's greatest strengths, and that you think of other characteristics first when you think of his preaching. The spread on originality in the Thielicke ratings was divided as follows in the four groups: (4) 21, (3) 19, (2) 17, (1) 25. This represents one of the most striking results of our study. Even though originality still stands slightly below the mid-point on our scale it must be considered as extremely important in any portrayal of the preaching of Helmut Thielicke. This, as we have seen, is clearly evident in a study of his sermons.

On the other hand, the fact that originality is less evident in the preaching of Woldemar Lein should not give us cause to disparage his preaching. General approval and appreciation of Lein's use of the Bible in preaching, his high rating in credibility, the recognition of the thought provoking quality of his sermons, and approval of his wide choice of subjects gives ample evidence that his sermons are worthy of attention.

The lower ratings given Thielicke on *use of the Bible* and on *credibility* do not necessarily indicate as much less appreciation of T in regard to his credibility and use of the Bible. These somewhat lower scores may reflect several conditions. First, they may reflect the great strength of T in other factors such as relevancy, personality, prophetic voice, and use of illustrations. Secondly, they may reflect certain subjective attitudes toward the Bible and toward preaching in general on the part of the main body of listeners in Germany. The fact that credibility was placed at the top of the Ideal Q-sort list by T Ls might indicate that to some degree T Ls are demanding more of the minister by way of credibility than does the average Methodist listener of our random sample of Christuskirche members. Conversely, one might argue that by placing use of the Bible lower on the Ideal list, the average T L expects less of the preacher in this respect and therefore finds his strengths in other factors.

Both T and L were rated high on *comprehensibility*. Our entire study gives evidence that laymen consider comprehensibility one of the most important factors in preaching.

Many of the people who ranked T high in *comprehensibility* made remarks such as the following. "What he says is not always easy to understand, but I can understand him." The writer suggests that a high mark in comprehensibility for the preacher may be, at the same time, a high self-rating on the ability of the subject to understand and a high mark for the preacher who makes himself understood. Only occasionally did a listener complain that T uses too many strange words (*Fremdwörter*). Some of the same subjective elements were undoubtedly operative in the evaluation of the comprehensibility of Lein's preaching, though to a lesser degree. Also, strange words appear much less frequently in Lein's preaching, and never without explanation.

Both men were rated about equally high on *theological content.* This factor was defined in lay terms to include Christian teaching (Christliche Lehre). In theological content, as defined by the laymen in this study, Thielicke rated the highest mean and the strongest modal choice in the *most important* column. For Thielicke no factor rated stronger approval by the laymen, even though for Lein credibility and use of the Bible rated higher scores.

When the means of the Thielicke and Lein Q-sort on preaching were combined we found that the factors with the ten highest combined means were the same as those in the list of the first ten of the Ideal Q-sort L E Fs with the exception of *confrontation with decision,* which in this list is found in the third quartile. The characteristic which is elevated in the Q-sort in preaching is *preacher's personality.* L Ls rated this factor in tenth place and T Ls placed it in fourth place. It seems that although listeners generally think that personality is one of the less important factors as compared to others in the Ideal Q-sort, when evaluating its position as related to the preaching of Thielicke or Lein interviewees almost invariably gave it a higher position. The tendency to do just the opposite with *confrontation with decision* is seen in the comparison of the two test results.

One additional factor in which T Ls noted strength in the preaching of Thielicke is the *use of illustrations*. As indicated in Graph II, along with *originality, preacher's personality,* the next widest divergence from the ranked expectation factors is Ts rating on *use of illustrations*. Even Thielicke's critics credit him with excellent use of illustrations. Our study shows that men are most intrigued with his illustrations, while women—especially housewives—accord him a somewhat lower rating on this factor.

One factor in which both T and L were ranked considerably lower in the Q-sort on preaching than on the Ideal Q-sort was *practical help for living*. This is evidently a difficult area for the listener to assess. That is, for the layman it is not easy to answer the question: How much does his preaching help me in my daily life?

At this point, in spite of the exceptions to which we have been calling attention, we conclude that the ranking of factors as shown in the Q-sort on preaching in Table 6 gives added weight to the importance of the Ideal Lay Expectation Factor list as representing a useful hierarchy of preaching values.

Since the Q-sort tests do not provide a qualitative evaluation of the strength of any given factor in the preaching of the men we are studying, as was suggested earlier, we need now to make use of our cross-check on the L E Fs in the form of the results derived from the General Preaching Characteristics Test also administered to each of the 137 laymen (see p. 32).

General Preaching Characteristics Test Results

The score resulting from the computations of this test is called the scale value rating (S V R). In the scale value rating process of this test the laymen were *not consciously comparing one factor with another.* As a result rank order is somewhat less significant than with the Q-sort tests. However, the fact that all the ratings tended to be high in this test has much to say about the preaching of Thielicke and Lein. Table 7, Page 269, shows a comparison of the S V Rs on the test items related to the 20 L E Fs in the preaching of Thielicke and Lein. In this table the contrasts stand out in bold relief. The Spearman rho rank order test yields a correlation of .01, which indicates a very limited relationship, and no significance at the 5% level.

However, although the contrasts in rank order stand out in bold relief, the actual differences between the high and low mean scores are small as compared to the differences resulting from the Q-sort ratings. This again gives visual evidence of the often heard comment of the listeners, "He does everything well." Visually this is perhaps even more graphically shown in Graph III, Page 270, in which scale value ratings derived from the G P C Test are plotted along with Thielicke and Lein Q-sort ratings from the second Q-sort.

The *scale value rating* lines show which L E Fs are *strong* in the preaching of the ministers studied, regardless of how important any particular factor was rated in the Q-sort. It seems almost superfluous to point out the *contrasts* between the Q-sort ratings and the scale value ratings, which the reader can check on Graph III.

The widest contrast between the two sets of ratings for both preachers is on the *use and basis of authority*. Note especially the exceptionally high scale value ratings for Thielicke on *practical help for living*, on *evidence of preparation*, on *use of illustrations*, and on *originality*. Other characteristics showing great strength here are *love-fear* (quality of motivation), *prophetic voice*, and even *range of subjects*, all of which had been placed under *less important* by a majority of the listeners in the Q-sort tests. The importance of these factors in the success of Thielicke as a preacher cannot easily be overstressed. To those who have read Chapter 5 in this book it will be no surprise that listeners feel that Thielicke comes into the pulpit well prepared to present his message. Although the reasons for high scale value ratings in *love-fear*, *prophetic voice*, and other factors may be somewhat less obvious, they are none the less convincing to the listener.

Table 7

SCALE VALUE RATINGS FROM 60 TEST ITEMS
Related to 20 Lay Expectation Factors
in the Preaching of Thielicke and Lein

THIELICKE LEIN

Mean Scale Value Rating

practical help	3.44	3.50	comprehensibility
illustrations	3.43	3.44	authority
preparation	3.41	3.31	continuity
thought provoking	3.31	3.30	theological content
attention holding	3.27	3.27	inspirational
relevancy	3.25	3.26	credibility
authority	3.21	3.21	Bible
comprehensibility	3.18	3.19	personality
originality	3.17	3.16	preparation
continuity	3.15	3.15	delivery
credibility	3.08	3.15	practical help
Bible	3.06	3.13	illustrations
delivery	3.05	3.07	attention holding
range of subjects	3.04	3.04	love - fear
theological content	3.03	2.99	decision
personality	3.01	2.93	prophetic voice
inspirational	2.89	2.91	relevancy
prophetic voice	2.89	2.90	thought provoking
love - fear	2.88	2.66	originality
decision	2.86	2.43	range of subjects

Source: Lay Expectation Factor Study, 1968, M. Dirks,
B.U.S.T.

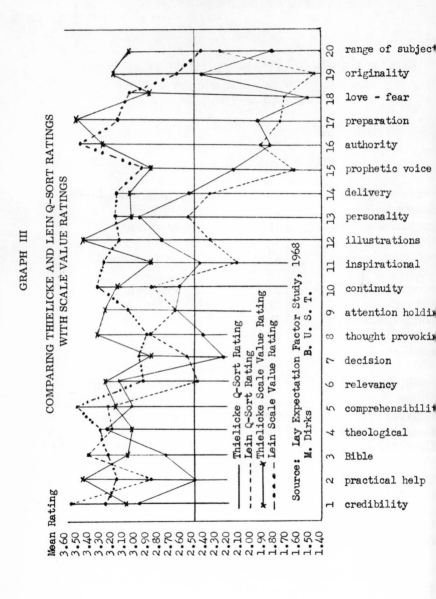

GRAPH III

COMPARING THIELICKE AND LEIN Q-SORT RATINGS
WITH SCALE VALUE RATINGS

Mean Rating

3.60
3.50
3.40
3.30
3.20
3.10
3.00
2.90
2.80
2.70
2.60
2.50
2.40
2.30
2.20
2.10
2.00
1.90
1.80
1.70
1.60
1.50
1.40

——— Thielicke Q-Sort Rating
– – – Lein Q-Sort Rating
—×— Thielicke Scale Value Rating
••••• Lein Scale Value Rating

Source: Lay Expectation Factor Study, 1968
M. Dirks   B. U. S. T.

1 credibility
2 practical help
3 Bible
4 theological
5 comprehensibili
6 relevancy
7 decision
8 thought provoki
9 attention holdi
10 continuity
11 inspirational
12 illustrations
13 personality
14 delivery
15 prophetic voice
16 authority
17 preparation
18 love – fear
19 originality
20 range of subject

In line with our purpose of reporting not only on one successful preacher (Thielicke) and his preaching, but also on a successful preacher in a control study we report that Lein listeners in the G. P. C. Test responded to his preaching with almost equally high scale value ratings. This the reader can readily see in Table 7 and on Graph III.

We have mentioned the ten listeners who were a part of both groups of interviewees. Computations on their Q-sort ratings show no significant differences from the rest of the sample in each case. On the G P C Test two striking results are evident. First, the *rank order* of the individuals and their scores on both tests are identical. Second, the S V Rs on Thielicke are higher in every case. However, the mean difference is only .25, which in this case is significantly small. Since the rank order was identical, the Spearman rho formula yields a perfect score of 1. This, of course, speaks only of the average total score given by each of the ten individuals. As to variations in the ratings on specific expectation factors by these ten interviewees, all the differences between T and L found in the total group of interviewees were exhibited. Thus the results from the ten did much to demonstrate the reliability of our findings.

The Response: Based on Occupational
Grouping—

In this section and others to follow the attempt is to be made at answering a number of related questions that come again and again to one attempting to relate and evaluate the characteristics of preaching (our lay expectation factors) to effective preaching. One form in which the question often comes is: Is there a substantial difference between groups in their expectations? In other words, who is affected most by what characteristics? Or for example, which groups, if any in particular, were responsible for Thielicke's high rating in *theological content* or in *inspirational quality?* Without attempting to list a host of similar questions we shall proceed to share with the reader some of the more striking differences as related to group responses. We begin with those related to occupational grouping.

General Preaching Characteristics Test results indicate that Managers and Craftsmen, followed by Housewives, gave the highest over-all scores to Thielicke on all 20 factors. Ministers (not laymen), followed by students, gave the lowest ratings, with Professional and Clerical-Office people near the mean.

On the Thielicke preaching Q-sort the *manager-craftsmen* group scored T highest on *theological content* with a 3.60. This is +.38 above the highest mean for any factor on this test, which happens to be on theological content.

The eight ministers in the sample rated this factor lowest at 2.50 or -.72 from the mean. The managers and craftsmen also gave high ratings on *inspirational quality,* but gave among the lowest ratings on *love-fear* (motivation), and on *preacher's personality.* The lowest rating on personality was given by the clerical-office group.

It became very evident that ministers differ most from all of the occupational groups in their criticisms and in their ratings. For the benefit of any minister who may be interested in the specific degree of divergence registered we list the most divergent ratings below. A plus or minus .34 or more is considered a significant difference.

-.83 credibility	+.84 delivery
-.75 practical help	+.70 use of illustrations
-.72 theological content	+.65 preparation
-.48 inspirational quality	+.47 attention holding
-.47 authority	+.47 thought provoking
-.46 use of the Bible	+.24 love-fear motivation
-.46 confrontation with decision	

On all of the remaining factors the ministers registered only small differences excepting a -.15 on comprehensibility which is hardly significant. Judging from the above it would seem that ministers are impressed by Thielicke's preparation (evidence of), and especially by his delivery and use of illustrations. They seem to be much less impressed than the laymen by his credibility, theological content, and ability to give practical help for living.

Students registered plus or minus ratings on the same factors as ministers but in much less extreme fashion. There was one notable exception to this tendency. Students generally recognized Thielicke as a *prophetic voice,* whereas ministers rated him near the mean on this characteristic.

The professional group, doctors, lawyers, professors, teachers, registered the lowest rating for Thielicke on *use of the Bible.* For this group 14 other characteristics were rated as more important in Thielicke's preaching. Their rating was, however, not much lower than that of the ministers on this characteristic. As was expected, the professionals scored Thielicke highest on *originality* and on *relevancy.* Students, professionals, housewives, and ministers scored originality above the mean and the, manager-craftsmen, clerical-office, and the retired and semi-retired groups scored originality below the mean. Professionals were most impressed with Thielicke's relevancy and housewives least.

Housewives scored a -.66 on use of illustrations by Thielicke. So where ministers and men in general were impressed by his use of illustrations, housewives found other characteristics more appealing. Housewives and the clerical-office group scored T highest on confrontation with decision.

Clerical-office workers registered the highest ratings on continuity and on prophetic voice. They gave the lowest ratings on originality with a -.66, and surprisingly registered one of the lowest ratings on preacher's personality.

Lest anyone think the ratings on *preacher's personality* to be related to the sex of the interviewee, professionals, housewives, and ministers scored preacher's personality above the mean, while the retired, managers and craftsmen, and clerical-office workers registered this factor below the mean for the 82 T Ls. The ideals which the preacher holds before himself in his preparation for preaching have much to do with the results reported above.

The Response: Based on Educational Attainment—

For the purpose of comparison the T L sample was divided logically into two groups: those who have graduated from the preparatory schools for university entrance and those who have not. The first group includes some persons who have completed graduate degrees as well as persons engaged in graduate study. The second group includes persons in a wide variety of occupations not demanding advanced study, many of whom may nevertheless be well-trained and highly skilled in their respective fields of interest. Some have an education comparable to an American grade or junior high school level.

The difference in expectation of preaching at

the "ideal" level between the high and low educational attainment groups are so significant
that it seemed useful to include Table 8, page
277, so that the reader can readily visualize
these differences for himself. Again to point
out what is obvious on the table, the more highly educated think that the *use of illustrations*
is among the less important factors. *Use of the
Bible* and *confrontation with decision,* although
ranked lower by the more educated, are nevertheless rated as "very important." Other differences in Table 8 the reader will note according to his interest.

On the Q-sort on the preaching of Thielicke
the largest differences in the ratings of the two
groups, as can be seen in Table 9, page 278, involve *use of the Bible, originality, theological
content,* and *use of illustrations.*

Here the more educated group placed the
use of illustrations in second place. This seems
to completely reverse their original judgment
in the Ideal Q-sort. We make note that the less
educated group places *use of the Bible* in a
much higher position than the more educated
group. Whereas in the Ideal Q-sort the educated
placed *theological content* in the "most important" position, in the Q-sort on the preaching
of Thielicke the situation is reversed. The less
educated have placed it at the head of the list,
while the more educated have placed it in fifth
position. As expected the more educated credit
Thielicke with a high rating in *originality,*

Table 8

20 IDEAL LAY EXPECTATION FACTORS
Ranked by 82 Thielicke Listeners Grouped
According to Educational Attainment

High Educational Attainment LEFs	Q-sort Ratings		Low Educational Attainment LEFs	Difference
credibility	3.59	3.56	credibility	-.03
comprehensibility	3.27	3.37	practical help	+.22
theological content	3.27	3.34	Bible, use of the	+.66
relevancy	3.17	3.07	decision	+.53
practical help	3.15	3.05	comprehensibility	-.22
thought provoking	2.93	3.00	relevancy	-.17
continuity	2.90	2.98	theological content	-.29
Bible, use of the	2.68	2.68	thought provoking	-.25
decision	2.54	2.51	attention holding	+.10
preacher's persnlty	2.44	2.49	inspirational quality	+.37
attention holding	2.41	2.37	delivery, manner of	+.10
delivery, manner of	2.27	2.34	continuity	-.56
prophetic voice	2.17	2.32	illustrations	+.69
inspirational	2.12	2.17	preacher's persnlty	-.27
originality	1.95	2.05	prophetic voice	-.12
authority	1.88	1.95	authority	+.07
preparation	1.78	1.88	preparation	+.10
love-fear	1.73	1.76	love-fear	+.03
illustrations	1.63	1.61	originality	-.34
range of subjects	1.46	1.46	range of subjects	.00

Source: Lay Expectation Factor Study, 1968, M. Dirks, B.U.S.T.

Table 9

20 LAY EXPECTATION FACTORS IN
THE PREACHING OF THIELICKE
Ranked by 82 Thielicke Listeners Grouped
According to Educational Attainment

High Educational Attainment LEFs	Q-sort Ratings		Low Educational Attainment LEFs	Difference
relevancy	3.15	3.54	theological content	+.64
illustrations	3.12	3.15	credibility	+.39
preacher's persnlty	3.11	3.09	relevancy	-.06
comprehensibility	2.98	3.07	comprehensibility	+.09
theological content	2.90	3.05	Bible, use of the	+.68
attention holding	2.85	2.76	preacher's persnlty	-.35
originality	2.78	2.73	practical help	+.46
credibility	2.76	2.59	continuity	-.04
continuity	2.63	2.49	illustrations	-.63
delivery, manner of	2.63	2.49	inspirational	+.03
inspirational	2.46	2.46	attention holding	-.39
thought provoking	2.46	2.44	delivery, manner of	-.19
Bible, use of the	2.37	2.37	thought provoking	-.09
practical help	2.27	2.32	decision	+.22
prophetic voice	2.24	2.12	originality	-.66
decision	2.10	2.10	prophetic voice	-.14
preparation	1.98	2.00	authority	+.32
range of subjects	1.83	1.98	preparation	.00
authority	1.68	1.85	range of subjects	+.02
love-fear	1.63	1.39	love-fear	-.24

Source: Lay Expectation Factor Study, 1968, M. Dirks, B.U.S.T.

while for the less educated this factor in his preaching is somewhat less important.

The results of the G P C Test show that the mean S V R for the more highly educated half of the sample is 2.88, while the S V R for the less educated is 3.25. This seems like a significant mathematical difference of .37. However, when one considers the fact that the more educated interviewees are accustomed to grading and rating procedures and as a result may grade more critically, this difference may not be a reliable indication of actual difference in appreciation of Thielicke's preaching on the part of the two groups.

When comparing the sermons of Thielicke with the sermons of other ministers on a ten-point scale, the mean rating by the more educated group was only slightly lower than for the less educated. The difference was not statistically significant.

In summary, the most divergent rating by the half of the sample of Thielicke listeners with high educational attainment was their low estimate of the *use of illustrations* as an ideal in preaching and their complete reversal of form in placing this characteristic second only to relevancy as "most important" in the preaching of Thielicke. A second highly interesting but expected difference between the two groups on the two Q-sort tests was on *originality* for which the reader may refer to Tables 8 and 9.

Considering these and other significant differences in the ratings of the two groups it is noteworthy that Thielicke is able to minister to relatively large numbers of people in both categories, that is, to people of both high and low educational attainment. This in no way precludes the fact that his preaching draws an unusually large percentage of people from the educated class. Moreover, one cannot avoid the conclusion that vast numbers of people in the less educated classes of Hamburg society are untouched by and largely unaware of Thielicke's preaching. In the more educated classes there is universal awareness of Dr. Thielicke even among those who have never or seldom attended a preaching service at Michaeliskirche.

Even though the difference in appreciation of the preaching of Dr. Thielicke based on educational attainment is very small on the part of the 82 T Ls interviewed, there are significant differences between them as to which expectation factors are important to their appreciation of his preaching. Thielicke's *use of illustrations,* his *originality,* his *personality,* and the *attention holding* quality of his preaching are significant factors in his ability to preach in such a way as to hold so high a percentage of educated people in his listening congregation. The less educated listeners see strength in his preaching in *theological content, credibility, relevancy,* and *personality,* as do the more educated, but rate him especially high in *use of the Bible,* and in *practical help for living.*

Both groups are, of course, affected by the preaching of Thielicke as a whole. Our analysis of factors affecting any one group of persons more than others should not be taken to mean that persons are affected by any one or group of factors in isolation from others. Thus, factors such as *originality* and *use of illustrations* in the preaching of Thielicke are undoubtedly important in maintaining the interest of the less educated even though they are more cognizant of other factors. The less educated are probably as much affected by the *personality* of Helmut Thielicke as are the more educated, even though they may be less aware of the fact. Also, Thielicke's way of dealing with the Bible in his preaching may be a large part of what the educated layman thinks of as his *originality.*

[1]To check the significance of this and following correlations see Elmer B. Mode, *Elements of Statistics* (Englewood Cliffs, New Jersey: Prentice-Hall, Inc., 1963), p. 311. According to Table O, entitled "Critical Values of Spearman's Rank Correlation," where N equals 20, a Spearman rho correlation as low as .59 would be significant at the .01 level.

Chapter 8

CONCLUSIONS

The pages which follow may be conceived as recapitulation or summary. However, certain new perspectives may be opened to the reader. Without being unduly presumptuous, let us begin with the assertion that a useful method for the study of factors involved in lay receptivity to preaching has been developed as reported in the preceding pages of this book.

Through the Q-sort method combined with the use of a General Preaching Characteristics Test administered in interviews with listeners to two men recognized as superior preachers, a comprehensive, though not exhaustive, list of factors involved in receptivity of the layman to preaching has been developed and tested.

The list of *Twenty Lay Expectation Factors* has been arranged into a hierarchy in which the comparative importance of the factors included has been indicated. This list as shown in Table 5, page 255 and in Graph I, page 257 must represent one of the significant results of the entire study.

The *Q-sort methodology* was found to be a useful tool with which to develop and test the lay expectation factor list and to determine the comparative importance of the basic factors underlying the response of the listener to preaching. By use of the Q-sort laymen were shown to be in substantial agreement on the primary importance of eight of the twenty factors as most significant in their response to preaching. After the eight factors there was a sharp drop in the ratings. However, we must quickly note that each of the twenty Lay Expectation Factors were considered as "most important" by two or more persons interviewed, and as "very important" by ten or more persons.

Moreover, there is a high correlation between the characteristics of preaching considered important by the laymen in an "ideal" sense and those considered by them as important in the preaching of a "successful preacher." As can be seen in Graph II the ten factors rated highest in the description of the "ideal" preacher by the laymen were also placed high in the ranking of factors in their description of the preaching of Pastor Lein and of Dr. Thielicke, men known as effective preachers.

Nevertheless, when the preaching of a specific preacher was described by laymen in terms of the Lay Expectation Factors there was a wide variation in the order of importance of the twenty factors. Thielicke preaching differs considerably from the "ideal" rating of factors in that he was ranked higher in *preacher's personality, originality,* and in *use of illustrations,* while at the same time receiving high ratings in factors high on the "ideal" list.

Pastor Lein's preaching, as described by his listeners, fits the pattern of the "ideal" preacher more closely but also varies from the ideal pattern with higher ratings in *range of subjects, continuity, personality,* and *use of illustrations.*

Factors rated below the "ideal" rating by the laymen in the preaching of Thielicke were *credibility, practical help for living, confrontation with decision,* and *thought provoking quality.* Lein ratings were lowered in *prophetic voice, relevancy, practical help for living,* and *confrontation with decision.*

In the early stages of the study of Lay Expectation Factors in relation to the preaching of Helmut Thielicke the writer hypothesized that the elements of preaching as assessed by laymen and represented by the twenty lay expectation factors would be shown to be positively dealt with in the preaching of Thielicke. This hypothesis was strongly supported by the entire study but especially by the results of the General Preaching Characteristics Test. In other words, it was in this test that we saw Thielicke receiving high ratings on all twenty factors.

We infer from this that successful preachers may be expected to respond to the challenge of preaching in such a way that all of the lay expectation factors are dealt with positively in the view of the listeners. In general, at least, this was found to be true in the preaching of both Thielicke and Lein.

Some Elements in the Success of Helmut Thielicke as a Preacher

Most of the elements in the success of Thielicke as a preacher which are closely related to his ability to fulfill lay expectation have already been referred to in these pages. Others may have been implied.

Among the most determinative elements making for success are his boundless energy coupled with devotion to the task of preparation for preaching. Evidence for Thielicke's thoroughness in preparation is seen in the fact that the highest positive rating in the General Preaching Characteristics Test was accorded by listeners to the statement "It is evident that much preparation goes into his sermons."

His broad background in theology and ethics, his method of developing the sermon, his use of the Bible, and his thoroughness in preparation together with other strengths in his preaching make it possible for him to preach in such a way that his preaching appeals to persons of widely varying theological positions. Although about half of his listeners occasionally disagree with Thielicke on some controversial issues, the large majority agree with the main emphases in his preaching. In this connection there is no doubt that the *textual-thematic* method of organizing and developing the sermon is an important element in the effectiveness and persuasiveness of Thielicke's preaching.

Listeners agree that the biblical message is given contemporary relevance in his preaching. The comparatively high ratings accorded Thielicke in both *relevancy* and in *use of the Bible* may be based on the fact that he gives the biblical message contemporary significance.

Listeners generally agree that his constant activity in the field of writing has had a salutary effect on the preaching of Thielicke. His tremendous effort in writing *The Ethics* must be cited as having contributed immeasurably to his preaching. One of the great strengths of his preaching may well be that he takes seriously his own advice not to "leap from the text into the sermon without having traversed the field of ethics."

There is special significance in the way Thielicke deals with the matter of *confrontation with decision.* The comparatively low rating accorded him on this factor may mean that the layman is not aware of the fact that he is being constantly confronted with decision in the preaching of Thielicke. The study of his sermons reveals that this element is exceptionally strong in his preaching. However, his way of preaching somehow brings the listener along from step to step so that he is responding affirmatively without being aware that he is being confronted with the necessity for making decisions.

One dominant impression gained from the study of his sermons is that he does not separate diagnosis and analysis from the remedy or from the solution as do so many preachers.

Although the results of this study show that the layman who is deeply concerned with *credibility* and *content* may be less concerned with the *preacher's personality,* in the response to the preaching of Thielicke there is strong indication that his personality is a prominent factor in his preaching.

One of the great strengths in his preaching may well be the fact that he has mastered the art of using a manuscript without giving the impression that he is reading. Although listeners say they are occasionally aware of his *style of delivery,* the large majority like his way of presenting a sermon. His practice of including the congregation in what he is saying by his multiple-use of the pronouns "we" and "you" is one of the important characteristics of his communication style.

The large majority of his listeners are aware of what we speak of as "dialogue between pulpit and pew" in Thielicke's preaching. In this connection our study shows that listeners who are aware of a high degree of "dialogue" in Thielicke's preaching are more aware of having their needs met than those who are less aware of "dialogue."

His preaching appeals to men as much as to women. Men, for example, like his *illustrations,* while women—housewives in particular—accord him a much lower rating on use of illustrations. He makes a point of preparing his sermons with the needs of men as well as women in mind.

The characteristic in which Thielicke differs most from the ideal ranking and also from Pastor Lein in the control study is in *originality*. A part of being original is "hard work." Whatever else it may be, a part of making preaching relevant demands the kind of originality Thielicke brings to his task.

It would seem sensible in any attempt to evaluate the preaching of Thielicke and to understand the response of laymen to his preaching that we take special note of those factors in his preaching which are rated by laymen in a manner diverging significantly from the Ideal rank order of the 20 lay expectation factors as portrayed on Graph II, on page 261. These peaks of divergence from the norm of the Ideal Lay Expectation Factors may well represent distinctions in Thielicke's preaching which have caused listeners to maintain their interest in that preaching throughout the years of his preaching at Michaeliskirche. To these factors and to the peculiar strengths in Thielicke's preaching we have already given considerable space in the previous chapter.

Only one added point under our present heading of "Some Elements in the Success of Helmut Thielicke as a Preacher" needs now to be stressed. It is that in line with the placement of *theological content* at the head of the list of lay expectation factors in the preaching of Thie licke, it should be stressed that the study shows that the laymen believe that Jesus is placed in a central position in his sermons. This was corroborated in our interviews and in observation. A study of his volumes of sermons further substantiates this conclusion.

Final Implications and Observations

We have said that a useful method of study of what laymen expect in preaching has been devised. It could be at the same time a method of studying the preaching of any given preacher. It has been suggested repeatedly that the usefulness of the methodology used in this study should be further tested in America.

To be sure, a pastor should give serious thought to the possible results of administering this kind of program of study of his preaching before submitting to such a study. In the Hamburg setting there was a sharpening of interest in the sermon in all its aspects from content to delivery, from preparation to the closing prayer. A number of interviewees witnessed that they had never been so interested in the sermon as in the weeks following the interviews. For many ministers the immediate effect would be felt as an inner demand for more thorough preparation of the sermon and possibly in a degree of increased self-consciousness in preaching. The self-consciousness would soon wear off; one would hope that the inner demand for more thorough preparation of sermons would remain.

For a preacher with a tenuous relationship to his congregation and an inability to respond favorably to the kind of challenge presented in the suggested study, the results could be distressing or even devastating. For the more secure person who is able to respond to this kind of challenge the results could be almost entirely salutary. Thus it would seem that before permitting himself, his preaching, and his laymen's expectations to become the object of study a pastor would want to take careful inventory of himself, of his willingness to learn and to change, and of other possible consequences to his ministry.

Ministers subjecting their preaching to the kind of analysis this study suggests might discover that the weaknesses in their preaching which they have heard most about are not necessarily the areas in which improvement is most needed. The reason for this is that listeners do not necessarily rate factors criticized lower than other factors which they may ordinarily not be willing or able to criticize. The real culprit may not be the obvious thing which is most often criticized. The study suggests that unless some such investigation of lay reaction to one's preaching is engaged in, he may not be challenged to discover and overcome those less obvious but highly determinative problems or weaknesses.

Certain observations that seem necessary at this point are related to the possible differences in the rank order of the *Ideal Lay Expectation Factors* that may emerge if and when the method used in this study is thoroughly tested in America. In our pre-study in America and in several incomplete studies conducted here since the study in Hamburg, interviewees seemed to be more "motivation" conscious but somewhat less concerned with credibility. It may actually be true that American listeners tend to trust their preachers more implicitly than do German listeners.

Americans interviewed also appear to be more concerned with whether the preacher gives evidence of adequate preparation. Some are especially concerned with the preacher's ability to hold their attention. At least these last two factors were placed consistently higher by Americans on the "Ideal" L E F list. One last contrast, Americans tested thus far seem to be less concerned with how the preacher deals with the matter of confrontation with decision; this factor has been given a "less important" rating by a majority of American interviewees. It would be interesting to know how the more prevalent *invitation* service here is related to this.

However, we must hasten to add that more extensive tests would be needed to substantiate or deny these possible differences.

Our study indicates that ministers hold a highly divergent view from that of the laymen of what is expected of them in terms of lay expectation factors in preaching. Moreover, the ministers' rating of the expectation factors in the preaching of Thielicke diverged widely from the rating of the laymen. Is it possible that studies are needed to discover how ministers conceive of the layman's view of what is expected in preaching? Would American ministers differ from American laymen in their evaluation of preaching as did the ministers in the Hamburg study? The crucial question, of course, is: Does the minister understand the layman's needs and expectations?

Some ministers may be afraid to let the layman minister to their needs as preachers in the way we have suggested in this study. This writer fully believes that the Church would make great strides if the layman's quest for credibility, for authority, for relevancy, and for what the layman longs for in theological content and use of the Bible were rewarded or could be more adequately rewarded by the minister's efforts in preaching. There is nothing superficial about the analysis of preaching on the part of many laymen.

A more determined effort should be made in theological education to make the preacher aware of the wide spectrum of lay expectation factors. Pastors are aware that the congregation expects a certain standard of excellence but they have not been subjected to the need for breaking this down into its essential and characteristic component parts. The study of lay expectation factors in relation to established homiletical procedures could be a helpful experience for theological students.

One thing is certain, a study of the life of Helmut Thielicke would be helpful to anyone whether interested in entering the ministry or not. Unfortunately no real life of Thielicke is as yet available, and even his *Auf Kanzel und Katheder* is not available in the English language. Men aspiring to become preachers could do nothing more profitable than to spend the necessary time to acquaint themselves with the dynamics behind the development of this peer of preachers and to study his sermons.

Finally, at the top of the "ideal" list of Lay Expectation Factors laymen have placed *credibility* and *practical help for living*. These two factors may represent the greatest needs in preaching and the requirements that are the most difficult for the preacher to meet. Both Thielicke and Lein have responded to the challenge of preaching in such a way that they have achieved a high level of satisfaction in these areas.

If Thielicke is correct in his judgment, and we have no reason to doubt him, then the major cause of our lack of credibility lies in our unconvincing Christian existence. This means

that behind the successful communication of
the gospel in preaching as in any area of Christian witnessing there must be first of all a convincing faith and a convincing life.

Appendix A

INTERVIEW INSTRUMENT

LAY EXPECTATION FACTORS

attention holding
authority, basis and use of
Bible, use of the
comprehensibility
continuity (organization) (orderly development)
credibility
decision, confrontation with
delivery, manner of
illustrations, use of
inspirational quality
love - fear (the quality of motivation)
originality
practical help for living
preacher's personality
preparation, evidence of
prophetic voice
range of subjects
relevancy
theological content (Christian teaching)
thought provoking

Cut into separate slips for use in Q-sort tests.

See supplementary definitions on pages 28 to 31.

299

300 LAYMEN LOOK AT PREACHING

Characteristics of preaching most often mentioned by laymen as basic to their response to preaching. Arrange in groups of five each as indicated:

MOST IMPORTANT

_____
_____
_____
_____
_____

VERY IMPORTANT

_____
_____
_____
_____
_____

IMPORTANT

_____
_____
_____
_____
_____

LESS IMPORTANT

_____
_____
_____
_____
_____

Characteristics are to be arranged according to their value in relation to your own personal response to preaching.

Which of the characteristics of preaching most often mentioned by laymen as basic to their response to preaching are most effectively included in the preaching of Prof. Dr. Helmut Thielicke?

Arrange them again in groups
of five as indicated:

MOST IMPORTANT

_____
_____
_____
_____
_____

VERY IMPORTANT

_____
_____
_____
_____
_____

IMPORTANT

_____
_____
_____
_____
_____

LESS IMPORTANT

_____
_____
_____
_____
_____

What Do We Anticipate in His Preaching?

The following statements are a part of a study of the preaching of Professor Dr. Helmut Thielicke, D.D. at St. Michaelis.

Think specifically of his PREACHING! You may have seen him in other activities, but let your answers here refer only to his sermons. YOUR OWN OPINION IS WANTED!

Please indicate what you yourself think in each instance. Your responses are anonymous. Do not sign your name. It is hoped that you will give your frank judgments.

Beside each of the following statements you find a row of small letters. These small letters, namely, a f o s n, represent a value scale of from "almost always" to "almost never."

Please mark with an x over only one letter of each row for the answer.

almost always / frequently / occasionally / seldom / almost never

a f o s n 1. His sermons help you gain new ideas and insights.

a f o s n 2. The biblical message is given contemporary relevance.

a f o s n 3. His concern for the church is evident in his preaching.

a f o s n 4. You feel that he has faith in the power of the Holy Spirit.

a f o s n 5. In his preaching he deals with a wide range of subjects.

a f o s n 6. In dealing with the scriptures he ignores the problems of interpretation.

a f o s n 7. He makes good use of repetition and restatement.

a f o s n 8. He relates the liturgy of the church to the message he preaches.

a f o s n 9. He supports the traditional religious values.

a f o s n 10. You feel that God speaks through him.

a f o s n 11. He uses theological terms without explaining them.

a f o s n 12. You agree with the main emphases in his preaching.

a f o s n 13. The point where he begins in his sermons is in the spirit of the times (the *Zeitgeist*).

a f o s n 14. He makes you want to refute him.

a f o s n 15. He seems to be preaching to you personally.

a f o s n 16. His sermons cause the listener to do some thinking on his own.

a f o s n 17. He explains the original setting of biblical incidents.

a f o s n 18. His sermons make theology meaningful to you.

a f o s n 19. Examples and illustrations help you to listen and remember.

a f o s n 20. His sermons are clearly organized.

a f o s n 21. In his sermons he deals with problems of daily living.

a f o s n 22. The way he uses the Bible in sermons seems highly appropriate.

a f o s n 23. His message can usually be easily comprehended.

a f o s n 24. His messages emphasize forgiveness more than guilt.

a f o s n 25. You have the feeling that he is using authority to lord it over you.

a f o s n 26. You discuss ideas from the sermon after it is over.

a f o s n 27. It is easy to "stay with" and listen to him.

a f o s n 28. Jesus is central in his sermons.

a f o s n 29. His sermons are built around a central idea.

a f o s n 30. His sermons make real the teaching that "God is Love."

a f o s n 31. When he is preaching I think about his style of delivery.

a f o s n 32. It is evident that much preparation goes into his sermons.

a f o s n 33. His personality detracts from his effectiveness in preaching.

a f o s n 34. His sermons introduce thoughts not ordinarily expressed.

a f o s n 35. His sermons indicate depth and profundity of thought.

a f o s n 36. His sermons show an awareness of people's practical needs.

a f o s n 37. His outline is difficult to follow.

a f o s n 38. You are often completely absorbed in what he is saying.

a f o s n 39. His sermons help you increase your knowledge of scripture.

a f o s n 40. He tends to "talk over my head."

a f o s n 41. He relates biblical teaching to the problem of daily living.

a f o s n 42. His illustrations are very interesting and stimulating.

a f o s n 43. You like his way of presenting a sermon.

a f o s n 44. His sermons inspire me to live nearer to God.

a f o s n 45. He chooses effective sermon titles.

a f o s n 46. You think there is adequate doctrinal basis in his sermons.

a f o s n 47. Distracting thoughts divert your attention during his sermon.

a f o s n 48. He talks *with* rather than *at* the congregation

a f o s n 49. He has experiences and insights worth sharing.

a f o s n 50. He holds your attention with his own earnestness.

a f o s n 51. He inspires me to be a follower of Jesus Christ.

a f o s n 52. He speaks of the power of the demonic in human life.

a f o s n 53. His use of humor is appropriate and refreshing.

a f o s n 54. He looks at his listeners as he speaks.

a f o s n 55. I disagree with him on controversial issues.

a f o s n 56. He sets himself to answer difficult and delicate questions.

a f o s n 57. The element of confrontation with decision is included in his messages.

a f o s n 58. His messages call for justice in community and national life.

a f o s n 59. His sermons inspire me to want a higher standard for myself.

a f o s n 60. He makes a point of making his preaching relevant and of dealing with the everyday facts of life.

GENERAL EVALUATION

(Circle the number on the continuum which represents your opinion. Ratings indicate from "10" among the best to "1" among the poorest.)

In your opinion, how do his *sermons* compare with those of other ministers?

10	9	8	7	6	5	4	3	2	1

How does he compare with other ministers in the *degree of intensity* of the message?

10	9	8	7	6	5	4	3	2	1

How would you rate him in fluency of speech?

10	9	8	7	6	5	4	3	2	1

How many times have you heard him preach?＿＿＿＿＿ times.
(You may approximate.)

CHURCH ACTIVITIES EVALUATION

Various church activities are listed below! Please circle the letter representing your opinion of the value of each activity with which you are acquainted.

(Acquainted means sufficient contact for you to form an opinion.)

very much	much	some	little	none	no contact	
V	M	S	L	N	NC	1. The Sunday worship service.
V	M	S	L	N	NC	2. Wednesday Bible-study.
V	M	S	L	N	NC	3. Women's society.
V	M	S	L	N	NC	4. Men's society.
V	M	S	L	N	NC	5. Young people's work.
V	M	S	L	N	NC	6. Sunday-school.
V	M	S	L	N	NC	7. Choir.
V	M	S	L	N	NC	8. _____

(Other organization.)

INFORMATION ABOUT YOURSELF

(This section is important to the analysis of the response to preaching. Please fill it out completely.)

Your Sex: _____Male _____Female

Your Place of Birth: ( ) under 1000 population
( ) from 1000 to 10,000 population
( ) from 10,000 to 100,000 population
( ) over 100,000 population

Your Age: ( ) under 18 Your Education: ( ) Volksschule
( ) 18-23 ( ) Mittelschule
( ) 24-35 ( ) Gymnasium
( ) 36-50 Final Examination ( ) yes ( ) no.
( ) 51-65 ( ) Trade or Technical School
( ) over 65 ( ) University (includes Hochschule)
Which completion-examination_____

Marital Status: ( ) Single ( ) Married ( ) Widowed ( ) Divorced

Church: Which "confession" do you belong to?_____
What is the name of your church? _____

How long have you been a member of this church?
Since _____

Your attendance ( ) almost always ( ) frequently
at worship ( ) occasionally ( ) seldom
services: (once a month)

Where else have you attended worship services? _____
_____

Have you held an office in any group or program affiliated with this church? ( ) yes ( ) no

Have you read books written by Dr. Thielicke?
( ) yes ( ) no
If yes, which books?
_____

In which Postal Division of the city do you live?_____

If not in Hamburg, in what place?_____

How long does it take you to go from your home to St. Michaelis?

      ( ) 15 minutes or less   ( ) 15 to 30 minutes
      ( ) 30 minutes to an hour ( ) more than 1 hour

How long have you lived in Hamburg?

      ( ) less than 1 year   ( ) 1 to 4 years
      ( ) 5 to 9 years   ( ) 10 to 20 years
      ( ) 21 or more years

Appendix B

LAY EXPECTATION FACTORS

Table 1

TWENTY LAY EXPECTATION FACTORS WITH NUMBERS
OF THE ITEMS IN THE GENERAL PREACHING CHARAC-
TERISTICS TEST RELATING TO EACH FACTOR

1. attention holding — 19, 27, 38, 42, 47
2. authority, basis and use of — 22, 25, 28, 48
3. Bible, use of the — 2, 6, 17, 22, 39, 41
4. comprehensibility — 11, 23, 40
5. continuity (organization) — 7, 20, 29, 37, 43
6. credibility — 2, 4, 10, 11, 12, 14, 18, 35, 40, 46, 48, 50, 54, 55
7. decision, confrontation with — 16, 51, 57, 58, 59
8. delivery, manner of — 7, 14, 15, 25, 27, 37, 43, 48, 50, 53, 54
9. illustrations, use of — 19, 42, 49
10. inspirational quality — 44, 50, 51, 59
11. love - fear (quality of motivation) — 24, 30, 51, 52
12. originality — 1, 34, 35, 45, 49, 56
13. practical help for living — 21, 36, 41, 49, 60
14. preacher's personality — 27, 33, 48, 50, 53, 54
15. preparation, evidence of — 32, 45, 54, 56
16. prophetic voice — 2, 58, 59
17. range of subjects — 5, 34, 45, 56
18. relevancy — 2, 13, 21, 36, 56, 58, 60
19. theological content — 3, 4, 8, 10, 18, 24, 28, 30, 35, 41, 46, 52
20. thought provoking — 1, 16, 35, 38, 45, 49, 56

Appendix C

THE POPULATION OF HAMBURG

Table 39

THE POPULATION OF HAMBURG ON JANUARY 1, 1965 — GROUPED ACCORDING TO AGE, SEX AND YEAR OF BIRTH

Age Groups	Year of Birth	Population on Jan. 1, 1965						For Every 100 Males ...Females
		male	%	female	%	total	%	
total		860 945	100	996 486	100	1857 431	100	115.8
under 1 year	1964	13,910	1.6	18,040	1.3	26,950	1.5	93.7
1 to under 3 years	1962 - 1963	25,948	3.0	25,070	2.5	51,018	2.7	96.6
3 to under 5 years	1960 - 1961	23,587	2.7	22,723	2.2	46,310	2.5	96.3
5 to under 6 years	1959	11,162	1.3	10,685	1.0	21,847	1.2	95.7
6 to under 10 years	1955 - 1958	39,338	4.6	37,515	3.7	76,853	4.1	95.4
10 to under 14 years	1951 - 1954	35,893	4.2	34,056	3.4	69,949	3.8	94.9
14 to under 15 years	1950	9,422	1.1	9,081	0.9	18,503	1.0	96.4
15 to under 16 years	1949	10,028	1.2	9,439	0.9	19,467	1.0	94.1
16 to under 18 years	1947 - 1948	21,157	2.5	20,446	2.1	41,603	2.2	96.6
18 to under 20 years	1945 - 1946	20,952	2.4	20,591	2.1	41,543	2.2	98.3
20 to under 21 years	1944	13,584	1.6	13,885	1.4	27,469	1.5	102.2
21 to under 25 years	1940 - 1943	66,003	7.7	61,789	6.2	127,792	6.9	93.6
25 to under 30 years	1935 - 1939	82,744	9.6	76,834	7.7	159,578	8.6	92.9
30 to under 35 years	1930 - 1934	57,636	6.7	56,587	5.7	114,223	6.2	98.2
35 to under 40 years	1925 - 1929	56,263	6.5	62,747	6.3	119,010	6.4	111.5
40 to under 45 years	1920 - 1924	52,450	6.1	72,327	7.3	124,777	6.7	137.9
45 to under 50 years	1915 - 1919	35,437	4.1	49,375	5.0	84,812	4.6	139.3
50 to under 55 years	1910 - 1914	58,098	6.7	76,436	7.7	134,534	7.3	131.6
55 to under 60 years	1905 - 1909	62,885	7.3	79,360	8.0	142,245	7.7	126.2
60 to under 65 years	1900 - 1904	58,125	6.8	71,440	7.2	129,565	7.0	122.9
65 to under 70 years	1895 - 1899	41,051	4.8	64,018	6.4	105,069	5.7	155.9
70 to under 75 years	1890 - 1894	29,387	3.4	50,712	5.1	80,099	4.3	172.6
75 to under 80 years	1885 - 1889	20,645	2.4	32,608	3.3	53,253	2.9	157.9
80 to under 85 years	1880 - 1884	10,643	1.2	17,276	1.7	27,919	1.5	162.3
85 to under 90 years	1875 - 1879	3,768	0.4	6,706	0.7	10,474	0.6	178.0
90 years and over	1874 a. before	829	0.1	1,740	0.2	2,569	0.1	209.9

*Brackets indicate heavy loss of males in World War I and World War II.

Source: Statistisches Jahrbuch, 1965 — Freie und Hansestadt Hamburg, Germany.

BIBLIOGRAPHY

Books

Baxter, Richard. *The Reformed Pastor.* (Edited by J. T. Wilkinson) London: The Epworth Press, 1939. Second edition revised, 1950.

Berlo, David K. *The Process of Communication.* New York: Holt, Rinehart and Winston, Inc., 1960.

Brack, Harold A. *Effective Oral Interpretation for Religious Leaders.* Englewood Cliffs, N. J.: Prentice-Hall, Inc., 1964.

Brigance, William Norwood. *Speech—Its Techniques and Disciplines in a Free Society.* New York: Appleton-Century-Crofts, Inc., 1961.

Brown, Roger. *Words and Things.* Glencoe, Illinois: The Free Press, 1958.

Bryant, Donald C. and Wallace, Karl R. *Fundamentals of Public Speaking.* New York: Appleton-Century-Crofts, Inc., 1953.

Budd, Richard W., Thorp, Robert K. and Donohew, Lewis. *Content Analysis of Communications.* New York: The Macmillan Company, 1967.

Clevenger, Theodore Jr. *Audience Analysis.* New York: The Bobbs-Merrill Company, Inc., 1966.

317

Davis, Henry Grady. *Design for Preaching.* Philadelphia: Muhlenborg Press, 1958.

Forell, George W. *The Protestant Faith.* Englewood Cliffs, N. J.: Prentice-Hall, Inc., 1960.

Hauptkirche St. Michaelis. Hamburg: Published by the Kirchenvorstand der Hauptkirche St. Michaelis, N. D.

Hayakawa, S. I. *Language in Action.* New York: Harcourt, Brace & World, 1941.

Hiltner, Seward. *Preface to Pastoral Theology.* Nashville: Abingdon Press, 1958.

Howe, Reuel. *Partners in Preaching: Clergy and Laity in Dialogue.* New York: The Seabury Press, 1967.

Howe, Reuel. *The Miracle of Dialogue.* Greenwich, Conn.: The Seabury Press, 1963.

Jackson, Edgar N. *A Psychology for Preaching.* Great Neck, N. Y.: Channel Press, Inc., 1961.

Mode, Elmer B. *Elementary Statistics.* Englewood Cliffs, N. J.: Prentice-Hall, Inc., 1961.

Monroe, Alan H. *Principles and Types of Speech.* Chicago: Scott Foresman and Company, 1962.

Mouly, George J. *The Science of Educational Research.* New York: American Book Company, 1963.

Rogge, Edward, and Ching, James C. *Advanced Public Speaking.* New York: Holt, Rinehart and Winston, Inc., 1966.

Schramm, Wilbur (ed.). *The Process and Effects*

of Mass Communication. Urbana, Illinois: University of Illinois, 1960.

Selltis, Claire, and others. *Research Methods in Social Relations.* New York: Holt, Rinehart and Winston, 1962.

Sleeth, Ron. *Persuasive Preaching.* New York: Harper & Row, 1965.

Spurgeon, C. H. *Sermons of the Rev. C. H. Spurgeon of London.* New York: Funk & Wagnalls, 1857.

Statistisches Jahrbuch, Freie und Hansestadt Hamburg. Hamburg: Published by the State Statistical Office, 1967.

Statistisches Taschenbuch, Freie und Hansestadt Hamburg. Hamburg: Published by the State Statistical Office, 1967.

Stephenson, William. *The Study of Behavior: Q-technique and Methodology.* Chicago: University of Chicago Press, 1953.

Stotts, Herbert E. *Church Inventory Handbook.* Boston: Wesley Press, 1952.

Thielicke, Helmut. *Das Verhältnis zwischen dem Ethischen und Ästhetischen: eine systematische Untersuchung.* Leipzig: Felix Meiner, 193—.

_____. *Geschichte und Existenz: Grundlegung einer evangelischen Geschichts-theologie.* Gutersloh: C. Bertelsmann, 1935.

_____. *Tod und Leben: Studien zur christliche Anthropologie.* Geneva: Verlag Oikumene, 1945.

_____. *Death and Life*. Philadelphia: Fortress Press, 1970.

_____. *Fragen des Christentums und die moderne Welt: eine christliche Kulturkritik.* Geneva: Verlag Oikumene, 1945.

_____. *Kirche und Öffentlichkeit: zur Grundlegung einer lutherischen Kulturethic.* Tübingen: Furche-Verlag, 1947.

*
_____. *Der Glaube der Christenheit: Unsere Welt vor Jesus Christus.* Göttingen: Vandenhoeck & Ruprecht, 1949.

*
_____. *Man in God's World.* New York: Harper & Row, Publishers, 1963.

_____. *Theologie der Anfechtung* . . .Tübingen: J. C. B. Mohr, 1949.

**
_____. *Der Nihilismus: Entstehung, Wesen und Überwindung.* Tübingen: Reichel, 1950.

**
_____. *Nihilism, Its Origin and Nature: With a Christian Answer.* Translated by John W. Doberstein. New York: Harper & Row, Publishers, 1961.

_____. *Theologische Ethik.* 3 vols., Tübingen: J. C. B. Mohr, 1951-58.

_____. *The Theological Ethics.* Vol. I. Edited by William H. Lazareth. Philadelphia: Fortress Press, 1966.

_____. *The Ethics of Sex.* Translated by John W. Doberstein. New York: Harper & Row, 1964.

_____. *Die evangelische Kirche und die Politik: ethisch-politischer Traktat über einige Zeit-*

fragen . . . Stuttgart: Evangelisches Verlagswerk, 1953.

*
_____. *Das Bilderbuch Gottes: Reden über die Gleichnisse Jesu.* Stuttgart: Quell-Verlag, 1957.

*
_____. *The Waiting Father: Sermons on the Parables of Jesus.* Translated with an introduction by John W. Doberstein. New York: Harper & Row, 1959.

*
_____. *Das Gebet das die Welt unspannt, Reden über das Vaterunser.* Stuttgart: Quell-Verlag, 1958.

*
_____. *Our Heavenly Father: Sermons on the Lord's Prayer.* Translated with an introduction by John W. Doberstein. New York: Harper & Row, 1960.

*
_____. *Die Lebensangst und ihre Überwindung.* Gütersloh: C. Bertelsmann, 1955.

*
_____. *Out of the Depths.* Translated by G. W. Bromiley. Grand Rapids: W. B. Eerdmans, 1963.

*
_____. *The Silence of God.* Introduction and translation by G. W. Bomiley. Grand Rapids: W. B. Eerdmans, 1963.

*
_____. *Zwischen Gott und Satan: die Versuchung Jesus and die Versuchlichkeit des Menschen.* Third ed. Hamburg: Furche-Verlag, 1955.

*
_____. *Between God and Satan.* Translated by

C. C. Barber. Edinburgh: Oliver and Boyd, 1958.
**
——————. *Offenbarung, Vernunft und Existenz: Studien zur Religions-philosophie Lessings.* Gütersloh: C. Bertelsmann, 1957. (Original edition was *Vernunft und Offenbarung,* 1936.)

——————. *Kleines Exerzitium für Theologen.* Hamburg: Agentur des Rauhen Hauses, 1959.

——————. *A Little Exercise for Young Theologians.* Translated by Charles L. Taylor. Grand Rapids, Mich.: Williams B. Eerdmans Publishing Company, 1965.

——————. *Die Atomwaffe als Frage an die christliche Ethik.* Tübingen: J. C. B. Mohr, 1958.
*
——————. *Das Leben kann noch einmal beginnen: ein Gang durch die Bergpredigt.* Stuttgart: Quell-Verlag, 1958.
*
——————. *Life Can Begin Again: Sermons on the Sermon on the Mount.* Philadelphia: Fortress Press, 1963.

——————. *Vom Schiff aus gesehen: Tagebuch einer Ostasienreise.* Gütersloh: Verlagshaus Gerd Mohn, 1959.

——————. *Voyage to the Far East.* Translated by John W. Doberstein. Philadelphia: Muhlenberg Press, 1962.
*
——————. *Wie die Welt begann: der Mensch in der Urgeschichte der Bible.* Stuttgart: Quell-Verlag, 1958.
*
——————. *How the World Began: Man in the First*

Chapters of the Bible. Translated with an introduction by John W. Doberstein. Philadelphia: Muhlenberg, 1961.

* —————. *Christ and the Meaning of Life*. New York: Harper & Row, Publishers, 1962.

* —————. *Von der Freiheit ein Mensch zu sein*. Tübingen: Rainer Wunderlich Verlag, 1963.

—————. *Was heist Freiheit?* Hamburg: Selbstverlag der Universität, 1963.

—————. *The Freedom of the Christian Man*. New York: Harper & Row, Publishers, 1963.

—————. *Das Schweigen Gottes*. Hamburg: Furche-Verlag, 1963.

—————. *Vom Geistlichen Reden*. Stuttgart: Quell-Verlag, 1961.

—————. *Encounter with Spurgeon*. Translation with introduction by John W. Doberstein. Philadelphia: Fortress Press, 1963.

** —————. *Deutschland, Demokratie oder Vaterland: die Rede an die Deutschen von Helmut Thielicke und eine Analyse ihrer Wirkung von Ekkehard Othmer*. Tübingen: Rainer Wunderlich Verlag, 1964.

—————. *Gespräche über Himmel und Erde: Begegnungen in Amerika*. Stuttgart: Quell-Verlag, 1964.

—————. *Between Heaven and Earth*. Edited and translated by John W. Doberstein. New York: Harper & Row, Publishers, 1965.

—————. *In America ist alles anders*. Hamburg: Furche-Verlag, 1957.

_____. *Der Eiselne und der Apparat.* Hamburg: Furche-Verlag, 1964.

_____. *Auf Kanzel und Katheder.* Hamburg: Furche-Verlag, 1965.

_____. *Leiden an der Kirche.* Hamburg: Furche-Verlag, 1965.

_____. *The Trouble With the Church.* Translated and edited by John W. Doberstein. New York: Harper & Row, 1965.

*
_____. *Ich glaube: Das Bekenntnis der Christen.* Stuttgart: Quell-Verlag, 1965.

*
_____. *I Believe: The Christian's Creed.* Translated by George H. Anderson. Philadelphia: Fortress Press, 1968.

*
_____. *Wie modern darf die Theologie sein?* Stuttgart: Quell-Verlag, 1967.

_____. *Sport und Humanität.* Tübingen: Rainer Wunderlich Verlag, 1967.

Tobias, Robert. *Preaching on Christian Unity.* St. Louis: The Bethany Press, 1958.

Walker, Helen, Lev, Joseph. *Elementary Statistical Methods.* Englewood Cliffs, N. J.: Prentice-Hall, Inc., 1961.

Wedel, T. O. *The Pulpit Discovers Theology.* Greenwich, Conn.: Seabury Press, 1956.

Windes, Russel R. (ed.). *New Series in Speech Communication.* Eight volumes. New York: Bobbs-Merrill Company, 1966.

Young, Pauline V. *Scientific Social Surveys*

and Research. Englewood Cliffs, N. J.: Prentice-Hall, Inc., 1956.

Zeuner, Walter. *Christuskirche*. Hamburg: Northwest German Conference of Methodists, 1959.

Unpublished Material

Parsons, Ronald John. "Lay Perception and Participation in the Communication of the Sermon." Doctoral dissertation, School of Theology, Boston University, 1966.

Ray, James L. "Factors Affecting Lay Receptivity to the Preaching of Ray A. Burkhart." Doctoral dissertation, School of Theology, Boston University, 1962.

Reid, Clyde H. "Two-way Communication in Small Groups in Relation to Preaching." Doctoral dissertation, School of Theology, Boston University, 1960.

Thompson, William D. "A Study in Church Audience Analysis." Doctoral dissertation, School of Theology, Boston University, 1960.

Articles and Periodicals

Berlson, Bernard. "The State of Communication Research." *Public Opinion Quarterly,* XXXIII (Spring, 1959).

Haiman, F. S. "An Experimental Study of the Effects of Ethos in Public Speaking." *Speech Monographs,* 16 (1949).

Katz, Daniel. "Psychological Barriers to Communications." *Annals the American Academy of Political and Social Science.* (March, 1947).

Lemsahl, A. S. "Die Hamburger sind keine religiösen Stumpfbolds." Article in the *Hamburger Abendblatt* (Hamburg), Jan. 6, 1967.

Michael, Rudolf. "Das Geheimnis eines grossen Kanzelredners: Tausend strömen zu Helmut Thielicke." Editorial in *Bild Am Sonntag* (Hamburg), Dec. 14, 1956.

Wilken, Waldemar. "Professor Thielicke und der Michel." Editorial in *Die Kirche in Hamburg* (Hamburg), April 23, 1967.

Zwischen den Zeilen. Religious Quarterly edited by Holger Hoffman. Flensburg, Germany: Published by Dieter Andresen, and others.

---

* Thielicke Sermons.
** Thielicke Lectures.

By a series of events which shall not be reviewed here but which today seem more than just happenstance it became the rare privilege of the writer to go to Hamburg, Germany to study lay expectation as related to the preaching of Dr. Helmut Thielicke. As a matter of fact, it was difficult at times to keep clearly in mind the purpose of devising and testing a method of study of *Lay Expectation Factors* from the purpose of learning from Thielicke whatever is to be learned from the preaching of a great and good man.

The fact that the writer had listened to much German preaching during his childhood and youth had something to do with his ability to pursue the study of *Lay Expectation Factors* in Germany. There were, however, four reasons why Thielicke was chosen.

(1) He has attained wide distinction as one who proclaims the gospel in terms understandable to modern man and as one who is concerned with communicating the living contemporary Word.

(2) His writings on widely different subjects and his printed sermons are available for study.

(3) It was thought that more could be gained from the study of the preaching of a man known as a highly successful preacher than from the study of a less successful preacher.

(4) Also, since Helmut Thielicke is not a pastor, the response to his preaching was thought to be more completely related to preaching than the response to the preaching of a pastor would be.